CW00672814

THE QUAREIA

APPRENTICE

STUDY GUIDE

by Josephine McCarthy

For more information, please visit www.quareia.com

Copyright 2018 © Josephine McCarthy

All rights reserved

Without limiting the rights under copyright reserved above, no part of this publication may be reproduced, stored in, or introduced into a retrieval system, or transmitted, in any form or by any means (electronic, mechanical, photocopying, recording or otherwise) without prior permission of the copyright owner and the publisher of this book.

Published by Quareia Publishing UK

ISBN 978-1-911134-32-9

Cover image by Stuart Littlejohn
Typeset and copyedited by Michael Sheppard

Contents

Introduction

When I first started writing the Quareia course, my intention was for it to be a simple first-stage training that people could then use to launch themselves into the hot waters of magic. However, the universe had different plans, and the course turned into a complete, long-term magical training akin to doing a university degree, and then some.

As the Apprentice section has no mentoring, it is the most difficult part of the training, and it has now become apparent that students need a bit of help here and there with basic questions, and with understanding certain concepts. I also felt that it would be helpful for Quareia students to have a better understanding of the dynamics behind the course and how it is structured.

This study guide is aimed at Apprentices studying the course. I hope it gives you a deeper understanding of the path you are walking, while also addressing a lot of the more common questions I have been asked by students.

It is not a 'cliff notes' type of guide; nor is it a bullet point summary of the Quareia course. Rather its intent is to shine some lights into the less obvious corners of your training. Hopefully it will help you along your path.

Josephine McCarthy.

What is a magician?
'One who does magic' is the Magician's reply.

What is a magician?
'One who stands at the centre of everything' is the Developing One's reply.

What is a magician?
'One who reflects the golden rays' is the Foremost One's reply.

What is a magician?
'One who is I,' replies the Divine.

Chapter One

How Quareia Works

Our virtues and our failings are inseparable, like force and
matter. When they separate, man is no more.

— Nikola Tesla

One of the first things to understand about a course as vast as
Quareia is how it works. This is more important that it first
appears, as knowing how a course works will tell you how best
to approach it.

Most people's experience of approaching a course is rooted
in high school and university education, and those learning
approaches are very different from a classical magical education,
just as they are different from any serious classical art form
education. So for many, the way this course is structured and
worked with will be a major learning curve. Many magical
schools, particularly self-learning courses, are written in ways
that reflect modern college learning techniques – and for smaller
courses that can work well. But for a full classical magical
education, the student is likely to run in to problems almost
straight away.

The Mysteries in any culture are complex and difficult to
learn. The aspirant is required to engage all their human skills,
not just their intellect. It is this need for drawing on every
aspect of yourself in order to move forward in magic that
many find difficult early on in their training. People are used
to compartmentalizing their learning, viewing it as something
separate from the rest of their lives. Also, their learning generally
consists of small bites taken out of various unconnected subjects.
The shift to total immersion into learning can prove difficult for
many, and impossible for some.

Properly studying magic requires hard work, some sacrifice, and the willingness to change and adapt how you think. And yet, though that sounds tough, it is one of the most rewarding, exciting, and fascinating journeys you can take through life.

It also requires that you be fully responsible for your own learning. In today's world of commercial teaching that has become the norm in many cultures—and in almost every aspect of learning, not just magic—students have become used to treating their education as a commercial transaction. As a result, they have developed an unhealthy attitude to their learning environment: they expect to be able to dictate to their teachers what they will learn and how they will learn it. Certainly, in some cases this has forced teaching establishments to smarten up; but overall, it has caused standards to drop as institutions water down courses, or tailor them to demand, or make them more 'appetizing' in order to attract more paying students.

While a young student may enjoy an easier, more 'fun' course that has been made tastier with appetizing but ultimately useless additions, in the long term the student will suffer from a lack of training, as the most important aspects of serious training in any subject are often the boring, difficult bits. On a deeper level, such a dumbed-down course disengages the ability of the student to learn effectively: they do not learn how to learn, but instead how to consume.

Some of the issues raised in this guide will be relevant to some, and not to others. Quareia is studied in many different cultures and countries, and in this book I have to address the various questions that have been asked from far-flung corners of the earth.

Some of the general queries I have been receiving, as students progress through this course, are issues I had not really thought about, but are quickly becoming apparent, hence this guide. Many of those issues are faced particularly by students who live in different countries around the world, issues that have to do with things like the difficulty of translating certain concepts or approaching the study of magic itself. There are also some simple yet annoying problems like broken links. I was stupid enough, when I started the Apprentice section, to quote web addresses. I was not thinking for the long-term about how links come and go, nor about the difficulties of accessing websites from certain countries. For that you have my deepest apologies.

In this chapter we will look at the underlying structure of the course, how it was built, why it was built that way, and what that means to you as a student. With that knowledge, you will be better able to understand the issues that come up for you in your study. It should also help you engage better not only with Quareia, but also with any classical magical training (and indeed any classical art form). In later chapters we will look at more specific issues, at various dynamics of learning, and at the most common queries that we have had.

1.1 The ethics and code of Quareia: Ma'at

At the foundation of the Quareia course is the philosophy of Ma'at, an Ancient Egyptian way of thinking that underpinned the whole ethos of Egyptian society, religion, economics and so forth. This philosophy was personified by the goddess Ma'at: the goddess of Truth.

I chose Ma'at as Quareia's foundation because it is the most stable, coherent magical dynamic out there. It will open the doors of magical and mystical understanding in their truest, deepest forms. Mysticism and magic become bedfellows as soon as you scratch below the surface of everyday magic. The deeper you get into powerful magic, the closer you step into mysticism.

Because Ma'at is so foreign to how our modern societies function and think, it may be worth spending a little time outlining this concept, as it is often misunderstood by modern minds. We tend, as humans, to relate and compare the unknown to what we know, and translations of unfamiliar concepts like Ma'at, which is often rendered in English as "justice" or "truth," can often confuse people further. Another translation of Ma'at in English is *balance*. Ancient Egyptian words, just like English words, often have various layers of meaning to them: what layer you pay attention to depends on context. (An example in English to make this clear: the word "spirit." This word can mean a human soul, the presence of the Divine, *any* supernatural being, boldness of character, a distilled alcoholic drink, and so forth. Most of the time, context makes it clear which meaning is meant.)

In English, our understanding of 'truth' and 'justice' are often coloured by our societal norms, our inherited religious beliefs, and our cultural patterns. If the two pans of a set of scales are in perfect balance to each other, this would be expressed in English as 'balance,' and in Egyptian, as Ma'at. In the Ancient Egyptian way of thinking, balance is truth, and lies express 'imbalance.'

Most magical students who look at Ancient Egyptian texts tend to concentrate on just two texts: *The Book of the Dead*, known to the Egyptians as *The Book of Going Forth by Day*, and a collection of late Greco-Roman Egyptian spells called *The Greek Magical Papyri*, which is a collection of magical spells that date from between the second century B.C. to the fifth century A.D.. Unfortunately, though these are very different texts from different periods in Egyptian history, both of them often lean more towards *Isfet* than Ma'at. Isfet is the disharmony and imbalance brought about by bad choices and actions, and the word is often mistranslated today simply as 'evil' or 'chaos,' terms that would be better applied to describe Apep, the chaos-serpent of the Egyptian mythos. (Also remember the earlier point about words having layers of meaning:

I am using the term *Isfet* here in the layer of its meaning which has to do with 'bad choices' and imbalance.)

As the outside influences of Greek and Roman culture increasingly ate away at the old ways of Egypt, so the sense of Ma'at retreated and the dynamic of Isfet emerged. This is particularly apparent in the Greek Magical Papyri.

This can all get very confusing for an Apprentice student. My advice is to approach all of this as you would any new subject: understand that there is far more complexity in the subject than at first appears, and the way to develop your understanding is to take small steps forward, one at a time. First learn the surface presentations of things, and the deeper aspects will emerge as and when you are truly ready to see them.

Ma'at is balance. This is expressed in Egyptian religious and magical texts as the balance of powers, and it was expressed in the code of the king and priesthood by the need to uphold the balance of powers, and also the balance of their day-to-day conduct. For the people, it was a simple code of ethical behaviour, a way of life, and a rule book that they could follow. So Ma'at had many different levels of expression, and all these levels are relevant and present in the Quareia magical training.

Ma'at was used both in the initial construction of Quareia and in the whole magical path that developed as a result. This was simply because it is the one philosophy that gets to the heart of how magic actually works, not because it comes from one particular culture. Ma'at is the dynamic that nature is based on, and the dynamic that allows the human to become an integral part of nature at a conscious level.

Ma'at is the harmony of cause and effect, of one thing rebalancing another, of the balance of light and dark, day and night, and of a harvest properly weighed and checked. As you progress through the course, you will be exposed more and more to the complexities of balance, both in magic and in nature. Every magical act has a counterweight to balance it out, and everything is upheld by the fulcrum of the scales. The fulcrum in magic is like a pillar that magic revolves around, and so long as everything is balanced out, the powers flow well.

Ma'at, or balance, gets to the very heart of magic, and once you understand this dynamic principle in action, then you will truly begin to understand magic. Ma'at is not an 'Egyptian thing,' rather it is an Egyptian word to describe a natural order in the mortal world.

You will notice, as you progress through the course, a lot of Egyptian magic and religious dynamics in the work. This is not because I favour Egyptian magic above all else, but simply because it is still, to this day, the most balanced and accessible profound magic that we can still work with and study. You will also come across lots of other different cultures and religions in the course, and that will be discussed in a later chapter. So let us move on and look at the various substructures in the course, so that you can understand why some things are put together in a particular way, and why some lessons are as they are.

1.2   The rule of absolutes

The rule of absolutes is a very old way of teaching that is still used occasionally in the teaching of classical art forms. When I was a ballet trainer who worked with professional and pre-professional dancers, I could always tell which of them had been trained using absolutes, and which of them had not. Those who had, displayed a solid technique and were able to grasp, absorb, and translate complicated movement concepts, and fully understand how those concepts related to their work. Those who had not, however, often quickly became confused, and could not easily absorb methods and concepts into their technique. The lack of absolutes in their training caused them to overthink and overanalyze their technique, which restricted their progress.

For my first couple of decades of teaching magic, I saw similar patterns in my students: a tendency to overthink and an inability to absorb what was necessary and integrate it into their work. It struck me then—I can be slow sometimes—that magic should be taught as a classical art: ballet or magic, the same foundational rules apply.

So what is the rule of absolutes?

The Rule of Absolutes is a method of teaching that includes barriers to contain each stage of the syllabus. These barriers allow the student to learn what is necessary at that point in their education without their consciousness constantly stretching forward and wondering what will come next. Students can focus purely on the step before them, and that becomes their world, their rule, their absolute. Once everything that is necessary has been absorbed, the barriers come down and the student progresses to a new phase of training.

A good analogy that I often use to explain this method is as follows: a toddler picks up a metal fork and goes to stick it in a plug socket. In the UK the voltage at a plug socket is 230 volts, which could kill a child. The mother takes the fork out of the child's hand, knocks their hand away from the plug socket, and says 'no' forcefully. The child is taught an absolute: they are not allowed to touch the plug socket. They do not know why, but they do as they are told.

When the child is about seven years old, the mother tells the child that the plug socket is dangerous, and they must never stick anything metal in it, as it could kill them. The mother then shows them how to plug something safely into the wall socket.

When the child is ten or eleven, the mother explains what the plug socket does, how the mains work, and where the fuse box is to turn off the electricity in an emergency. She then gets her child a kids' electricity kit, so they can learn to wire a board and make a light bulb come on.

As an older teen, the child learns in depth how wiring works, what its dangers are, what a ring main is, what amps are, how to change plugs, what happens with electric shocks, and how to administer first aid.

The 'absolute' for the child at seven is that the wall socket is dangerous and must never be played with. They don't know exactly why or how it works, but they know to stay away from it. As far as they know at that point, they must never, ever touch it, *ever*. Pertinent information is given at each stage of the child's development without swamping them with information they cannot understand.

This teaching method can be applied in many different ways, and for lots of different reasons. In Quareia it is deployed a lot, particularly in the Apprentice section and to some degree in the Initiate section. The student is contained by an absolute "this is it!" or a black and white, immovable rule, to allow their current stage of understanding to properly grow and deepen. Then, later, this boundary is removed, and they are exposed to another layer of understanding. This enables the student to take sure and solid steps, forming a foundation they can stand on, and their understanding and magical evolution grows at the pace that is right for them.

Succeeding and learning within a containment is rewarding: you have a limited pot of learning to achieve, an achievable goal, and a nugget of knowledge that you did not have before. Learning in defined steps is what develops an artist, not sitting in front of a piano railing at having to do your scales, frustrated that you cannot learn to play Chopin's works in a week. Learning to master the scales while taking pleasure in that ability is the reward of the absolute. It is the path, not the destination, that gets you there.

1.3   Repeat repeat!

True classical training is taught in a repetitive manner, and in a manner of *return*, and this method is also deployed in Quareia. In the early days of their Quareia training, the apprentice has many exercises that they must repeat *ad nauseam*, to the point of, at times, utter boredom.

This is not done to bore the pants off the student, but to get them to achieve two important things: one is to get rituals, exercises, and recitations into the deeper part of their mind. They stop having to think consciously about them and can do them without thinking: the actions become *engrammed* into their consciousness.

Engramming through rote learning is one of the foundational skills of magic, and it must become second nature so that it can be called on suddenly in times of need. First you must learn the skill of engramming, how it works, and what it feels like. Once you have practised that skill in some basic exercises, you can then choose to deploy it later in the course as and when you feel it is necessary.

The second skill that repetition teaches is patience. Being able to focus on something and to repeat it and practice it until you have become competent in it builds inner 'grit.' You get used to persisting with something, even when it is difficult, until you have achieved what you need to achieve. This is another necessary skill in magic. It is often overlooked, and yet it is a cornerstone of the craft. Being able to step up, practice, and repeat, even when you don't feel like it, silences the side of you that wants a constant input of new, glittery, and interesting things, and awakens the side of you that builds determination, forbearance, and discipline.

A magician without discipline is no magician at all: they are simply playing at it. The skill of discipline is critical to so many aspects of magic, and it must be present not only in one's actions, but also in one's thoughts and emotions. The mind is a major player in magic, but it is not matured by focusing directly on it. Rather it is strengthened and matured as a side effect of other work. The dynamic of one thing being strengthened by working on something not directly related is another major aspect of early magical training. It also plays a large part in other classical arts. In ballet, few students realize that the passive limb is actually being strengthened when that passivity is approached in a certain way. Dancers at the barre work first on one limb, then on the other. While the left leg 'works,' the right standing leg is being strengthened, if the training is correct.

All these threads of foundational training are woven together to create a solid base on which the magician can stand. Every lesson, and every aspect of a lesson, has all these elements woven into it.

1.4   From the outside in

The teaching approach to magical rituals, visions, and patterns is 'from the outside in.' First the student learns the outer aspect of a magical act, and they perfect that first before they step into any power at all.

Every magical act has two parts: the structure, and the power that fills that structure which essentially turns the magic 'on'. To stay with the electrical wiring analogy, first the wiring is laid, the fuse box is put in place, and the switches are mounted to the walls. Then they are all linked together for the power to flow through them. Then the power is switched on.

Similarly, the Quareia student builds a structure of magic within them before they access any level of power that could harm them. This structure-building also teaches them, passively and without them realizing it, that any magical trainee should have a basic vocabulary and structural understanding before they are introduced to power or contact. This understanding does not come from book reading; it comes from learning practically the early basics of magic such as rudimentary tarot and astrology, rituals with no contact or power, moving around in vision without leaving the mundane world (which some people call remote viewing), and so forth.

So the beginner develops a basic vocabulary of divination, ritual, and vision, the three foundation skills, and that slowly builds up to a solid basic understanding. As the student progresses in their training, power begins to flow into those foundation skills and fills them. In the Adept section there comes a point where the student starts to realize that once you have a solid competency in the foundation skills, the outer structure of those skills becomes less rigid: they become more fluid, more flexible.

This leads the magician to the understanding that once the structure and rules are learned properly, they can strike out and develop their own forms and methods of work. If a student attempts this too early in their training then they will flounder, as they are not anchored properly in the work. They will not fully understand the deep dynamics behind a unit of work or a method, which will make them vulnerable to damage and even catastrophe. In magic, as in any classical art, you must learn the rules and structures before you can learn to break them successfully. And that is the point at which evolution occurs in magic, and in any classical art.

Too often these days in any form of serious education, people reject or throw away their rules and structures far too early. This creates a dumbing-down of the system, and it ends with the blind leading the blind.

So this course is heavily structured towards the apprentice learning the foundations, learning the patterns, the basic rituals, etc., without power being connected to them. Later the outer patterns become more complex, and this pushes the student really learn how to 'pattern make'—which is to say, to create and work with rituals. Once this skill is in place, the work is connected to contact and power. Later in the course the student is shown how to connect with ever-deepening powers and contacts. If they have truly worked with the system as directed, then they will be ready for everything to switch on, and for the power to truly flow.

However, it is also important that right from the early days of a student's training they understand what power and contact feels like. So the rituals and visions they learn are not empty: they do have passive contact and power within their framework. Though the apprentice magician cannot yet trigger that power and contact for themselves in any depth, that contact and power does wait on the thresholds, and some of it washes into their work.

1.5   The three stages

The three stages of the training—apprentice, initiate, and adept—are not just labels, nor are they there simply to divide the course in three. They are three distinct phases of development in magical training: being torn apart, being reassembled, and finally 'rising in wholeness.'

In magical terms, this follows an ancient inner pattern: before someone can truly step into the stream of magic, everything within them that no longer serves a purpose—all weaknesses, vulnerabilities, and immaturities—must be stripped away. This is not done by focusing on those weaknesses; rather the apprentice's work triggers deep and ancient patterns of power that flow into their life, often unseen, and find every weak spot in them.

The Apprentice

The magical work done as an apprentice, besides learning outer structures through practice, is also a series of catalysts. Because the student has no real access to magical power, they have no control over the process. This really speeds up their fate and maturation and prepares them for the power they will step into as an adept. In a mundane life, it usually takes a lifetime, sometimes many lifetimes, to develop such maturity. But the moment anyone steps onto a serious magical path of training, that process speeds up. Lessons in life are learned quickly, and if the apprentice steps up to the process and realizes what is happening then they can engage with each situation that arises, and know that it a necessary process.

This can manifest in an apprentice's life in many different ways, depending on their weaknesses. It can trigger illnesses to slow them down and make them change how they live their lives, what they eat, what they do, etc. This is linked to a dynamic I call the *Pots of Resources*, which I will discuss in a little while.

The triggers in the Apprentice section can change where the student lives, who they live with, what they do for a job, where their interests lie, or how they behave as a human being. Regardless of how the catalysts affect the apprentice, once they understand that what is happening to them is a necessary process and stop fighting it, and rather engage with it, then they find themselves at the end of the Apprentice section, a bit battered, but wiser for the experience and in a better, fitter place. It is like cleaning house: all the rubbish is thrown out and the windows are cleaned, and the place is washed down, fixed up, and properly prepared for what comes next.

This dynamic also filters out those who have no place in magic.

Three main types of people are drawn to magical training. The first type came into life with magic in them: they have done it before, in some other life, and have come back to remember, advance, and mature into deeper magic. The second type are new to magic, but have been prepared, again through other lives, and it is a path that burns like a creative fire within them. Both these types are born to be magicians, and one way or another they will find their way through magic, regardless of the path they take.

The third type is a person fascinated by magic, but not truly able to take up its burdens. This is a long, tough, and often unforgiving path, but it polishes you from a rough stone into a diamond. But some people are unable to cope with the rigours of magic, or they are too unstable to cope with the power that flows through it.

The apprentice training, the 'being torn apart' part of the course, will unravel the third type out of magic for their own protection: fate will block them from it. One of the functions of the apprentice training is to act as a filter against those who are not suitable, for whatever reason, for deeper training. It will also block a person from stepping deeper into magical training until the right time comes. Timing is everything, and there are times in our lives when putting magic into the mix is not such a good idea. But when a student is really ready to try on the heavy mantle of magic, then the blocks will disappear and the path will open up.

This is an ancient way of training magicians: those who truly need to walk the magical path may have moments of being discouraged, of feeling overwhelmed, but they will not give up, or they will pause and return when they are ready.

Before I go on to talk about the processes of the Initiate and Adept sections of the course, I want to talk briefly about what I call *Pots of Resources*. From a magical perspective, each person has, at any time, a finite amount of energy 'stored' in different aspects of their lives.

To make this easier to understand, I always talk about various 'pots' of resources such as 'the pot of health,' 'the pot of magic,' 'the pot of emotions,' and 'the pot of the home' (food, housing, money). Over the decades, as I have observed my life and the lives of other magicians, I have noticed that if you use too much of the energy in one 'pot' and it is important that its store does not run out, then it will start to draw energy from the other 'pots.'

So for example, if you are engaged in a long round of powerful but necessary magic and you exhaust your 'magic pot,' then it will start to draw from your health 'pot.' This is often seen in magicians who commit to magical service at a powerful level: their health starts to suffer as energy is repurposed for their magic.

How fate and our actions affect the distribution of our energies is a complex topic, too complex to get into here. Suffice to say that one of the functions of the Apprentice section is to teach a person about their 'energy pots' through direct experience as opposed to theory. You will learn where your strengths and deficits are, and with this knowledge, you can walk your path wisely and healthily, employing the fullest reserves of your fate.

Finally the apprentice stands on the threshold of the Temple of the Mysteries and request entrance to the outer court of the true Mysteries. Many modern magical schools these days consider the very basics of magic to be 'outer court' training. In fact, that level of work does not even approach the steps of the threshold of the outer court. The reason for learning those basics first is to prepare the student to stand at the threshold of the outer court of the Temple of the Mysteries and request access. Only when the student is properly prepared will the threshold appear. At that point the student has to decide if they are really willing to take that step. Once one crosses the threshold of the

Temple of the Mysteries and enters its outer court, there is no going back to a mundane life. Even if you decide to cease your magical training and leave magic behind, if you have crossed that threshold then magic and the Mysteries will follow you wherever you go. It is a step towards the Divine, and a deep awakening: what has been awoken can never be truly put back to sleep. So the apprentice student who stands before that threshold is challenged to consider whether this is truly what they wish to do, and if they are willing to take up that mantle.

The Initiate

In the Initiate section of the course, the student steps out of the ashes of the Apprentice section and begins the process of being put back together. As they learn the knowledge and skills necessary for a true initiate of the Mysteries, they are also given the tools and skills to heal and rebuild themselves, and the strength to forge forward to the threshold of adepthood. When the initiate reaches the cusp of their adept training, they will be able to look back at their apprenticeship and see how everything that happened to their lives was necessary for things to have worked out as they did.

The path of the magician is the Path of Hercules indeed: it takes courage and strength to forge forward in the face of adversity, and this process polishes the student in every possible way. The Apprentice section is a tough one indeed, not because of the outer study, but because of the inner transformation that comes from that work. That inner transformation that happens as a result of the apprentice work prepares the ground and foundation for the house of the initiate to be built.

What was willingly relinquished as an apprentice is now transformed and returned to the initiate in a new and better way. What was withheld from the apprentice is released, and the final act of the initiate, as they stand on the cusp of adepthood, is to be reborn. The apprentice section is the death of the old; the initiate section is the conception, pregnancy, and finally the birth of the new.

The Adept

The Adept section of the training is where the magician truly steps into the Temple of the Mysteries and begins to learn the skills necessary to be accepted within the inner court: the company of the deities and the Justified Ones.

The Adept section takes the reborn one and trains them in the skills and knowledge of the adept. It weaves together the mystical and the magical, and puts the student in the midst of many of the aspects of the magical Mysteries so that they *become* those Mysteries. It is the direct experience of something that teaches you, not the study of theory.

As an adept student, the magician begins to realize the complexity of magic and the Mysteries, and begins to understand the enormity of the Mysteries: you can work for a lifetime in the magical Mysteries and still only scratch the surface. Once the adept has the skills, tools, and knowledge to properly face true power, they are cast into that power while confronting themselves. There must be no hidden weakness within an adept. We are all human, and we all have weaknesses and strengths, but the adept knows themselves: you know your weaknesses, which ones can be strengthened, and which cannot. You know how to compensate for any weakness, and even how to turn them to your advantage when necessary.

The difference between a mundane person and a true adept is that the true adept strengthens every weakness they can, and knows which weaknesses cannot be changed and must therefore be integrated into their life and personality. Hence the ancient maxim of the Mysteries: Know Thyself. In Latin this is *nosce te ipsum*, and in Greek γνῶϑι σεαυτόν (*gnōthi seauton*).

The final aspect of the adept training is stepping from the last remnants of the mundane and being born again into the life of the Justified adept. This title, and its attendant form, is to be completed at the death of the adept. The completion of the adept training is the beginning of the magical mystical life, where you have all the knowledge, tools, and skills necessary to walk a magical and mystical life in service.

1.6   Circles within circles

One of the major aspects of classical training is the *circling* of knowledge. Each part of magic has many hidden depths and layers. Just when you think you have learned everything you need to know, another layer reveals itself and you find yourself back on your journey of experimentation and learning.

This can confuse or trip up students who approach magic with a 'tick box' mentality: studied that, got it, now I move on. Magic and the Mysteries do not work like that. Each form, aspect, and dynamic of magic has endless depths which, when studied in depth and worked with, repeatedly reveals yet another layer. The surface layers are only the basic 'magical knowledge.' Beneath them are endless hidden layers that can take you into the adept aspects of your studies, until you reach the Deeper Mysteries.

Once you arrive at the layer of the Deeper Mysteries, a lifetime of discovery awaits you. As you mature and evolve, those levels of Mystery will reveal themselves as and when you are ready to integrate them into yourself. And so it goes on, layer after layer. At some point the adept mystical magician realizes that you can never reach the bottom of the pot of learning.

Each aspect of magic has many different faces, and behind those faces are the complexities of the weave of fate, time, power, and consciousness. On their journey, the magician realizes that the True Mysteries are not about histories, systems, beliefs, rituals, or religions. The True Mysteries are the same the world over, and they can be penetrated and understood only through inner transformation.

This is why classical training in any major art form is taught in a circular manner, or a *manner of return*. First the apprentice learns about the top layer of a subject by looking at it, touching it, 'sniffing' it: tentative exploration. As the student develops, matures, and gains knowledge and direct experience they circle back and reexamine the subject. This process of returning to a subject and looking further and deeper is neverending: it continues throughout a magician's training and throughout their life as an adept.

Quareia approaches magical training in the same way. The student, at each stage of their development, circles back to a subject they have already looked at and examines it more deeply, with more mature eyes. Over the many years it takes to complete the Quareia course, the student begins to realize that every aspect of magic and the Mysteries is indeed a bottomless vessel that can be reexamined throughout a lifetime. An adept should constantly be rethinking and reassessing what they believed were certainties, so that they are constantly evolving and developing as a magical being: they become The Developing One.

When the two opposing methods of Absolutes and Circling are brought together in training, they create a tension of learning, a balance of two dynamics that can at first confuse a student, but which will ultimately give them a mind that is flexible, astute, and grounded.

1.7   The good and the bad

Magical training in the West has mostly become an unbalanced education of 'only good' (or 'only bad'). This applies on many levels, but in terms of course structures and syllabuses, what has happened is that the student is only exposed to all 'good' experiences in their practical work. While this makes for 'happy consumer units,' it does nothing to prepare students for the onslaught of real magic, what it entails, what can happen, and most importantly of all *what it feels like, for both good and bad.*

Magic is an experiential art form, not a collection of spells and knowledge. Magic works with raw powers that can hurt you and beings that can trick and even destroy you. What keeps a magician safe through their developmental years as a student is not muttering banishing spells at every shadow, but the deep inner radar that they should be developing. And that can only develop from direct experience. The sanitizing of magic is another byproduct of the commercialization of magical training which has slowly crept in over the last few hundred years.

Everything now has to be a positive experience to 'keep' the student. And the root of the problem is wishing to keep the student, either for ego or for money. It is absolutely vital that a teacher never tries to keep a student; rather the teacher must give the student the best possible magical education they can. Whether the student stays or goes must be irrelevant to them. This means giving the bad with the good.

This dynamic of giving the bad with the good is not mentioned in the course, but it is there. I thought for a long time about the wisdom and implications of revealing this dynamic to students, as doing so can somewhat affect their resolve, and may prejudice how they approach their training. But given the rapid worldwide decline in educational delivery and the increasingly destructive and dangerous atmosphere now making itself known in various countries, I felt that it was probably, on the balance of things, more useful to outline this than to stay silent.

Eighty percent of the course's work is practical, and the student is given tasks to complete. Some of these tasks are directly magical, and some are not. Once the student has got some way into the course and has a good foundation of apprentice and initiate skills, then the course switches gears and sets tasks in a different way. The early stages of the course put a lot of magical protection around the apprentice, and the steps they are given to take are safe, secure, and will trigger an experience of one kind or another.

Once they reach the Initiate section, the training wheels start to come off, and the dynamic of bad versus good is slowly eased into the work. The student is given projects or tasks to do, some of which, while not dangerous, may or may not trigger experiences that are not exactly healthy in magical terms. This is not explained; rather the student is simply told to do such-and-such for some number of weeks.

The tasks and projects themselves are valid magical acts, and the skills learned are invaluable, but it is important for the student to learn how a repeated act over time can change. The nature of the contact can change for good or bad, and the energy can change for good or bad. When the student starts to feel more and more negatively affected, they are eventually driven to fall back on something they learned in their apprentice training: divination. They will check to see what is going wrong. This way, they learn what something feels like, they learn how to make a decision when they do not know all the variables, and they learn what it feels like when a situation is corrected.

Such experiences are invaluable. A physically unpleasant experience is something you never forget. But the student must never try to avoid such experiences: rather they have to learn what they can take and what they cannot, and to act accordingly. I do not exaggerate when I say that such experiences can save a life later on. They are necessary and an important part of the training.

They also teach the student something which is increasingly lacking in modern education and general wisdom: *anything* can be poison, it all depends on the dose. The same is true in magic. Because of the commercialism in the West and the concurrent dumbing down of our education systems, people are growing up with a very black and white view of the world. They think that if they pop a vitamin every day without fail, then they will be healthy. But some vitamins can be toxic if they accumulate. More is not better, and the idea of thoughtlessly doing the same thing every day has no place in magic. A magician must learn to weave their way through the path of fate. This is a complex skill to learn, as fate's dynamics flow through every aspect of a magician's life, from what they eat and where they live, to what magic they are doing at any given time.

The student will learn this through trial and error in their work, and they will learn it by their magical actions in training. After the first few experiences of this kind, they will start to realize that there was always a very quiet voice of warning within them, or a feeling of slowly building imbalance like a whisper slowly getting louder. The moment they recognize this is the moment they discover their own inner alarm system. That learning alone is the most precious thing in magic.

This method of teaching is not used in the visionary work, as it would be far too dangerous. Of all the aspects of magic, focused visionary work is the one that can truly open powerful doors, and because of that, the student is exposed only to those visionary structures that will help them grow and strengthen.

In terms of the further reading suggested for the student, however, a similar dynamic of good and bad is employed. There is little actual outside magical reading matter that is part of the course study, which can confuse students who feel that to learn magic, you need to read lots and lots of magical books. This is not correct, for many reasons, one of which is that a student who constantly dips into the all-you-can-eat buffet of modern magical writing can end up very confused. Certain magical texts are studied, some in depth, but mostly the student is given ancient Greek, Roman, and Egyptian texts to explore (they are also given supplementary research tasks on world cultures, myths, and religions). These texts are the foundations of Western magic, and they are still strongly relevant.

The 'bad' side of the scales, in terms of reading material, manifests in two ways, and only in the adept section, as the student needs to know enough of the rules before they can spot these underlying dynamics. One way is to expose the student to magical writing that 'is' magic: the text itself becomes a magical embodiment of power, and as such becomes its own consciousness. This is an ancient form of guardianship: the book acts not only as a vehicle for knowledge, but also as its own guardian. Poke it the wrong way and it will bite you.

The other way is to suggest that the student read one or two texts that are, basically, magical gibberish. It is important for the student to be exposed, without prejudice or teacher comment, to an example of a type of magical writing that is still produced today. This is work that is commercially driven, has little real magic in it, and simply repeats older texts that were themselves repeating texts invented simply to part superstitious and ignorant readers from their money. It is important that the adept student discovers this for themselves: they must develop their nose for bullshit and dressing-up, and learn to draw conclusions based on their own knowledge and experience. This cannot happen much before the Adept section, but once you are skilled in an art form, you can quickly spot inferior and counterfeit work for yourself. This is an invaluable lesson for a magician, for discernment is an important tool.

1.8 Learn the rules first

This is one of the most ancient principles of any classical training, and again it runs contrary to how a lot of people think today. You cannot break the rules until you know them completely, and thus know why you are breaking them, what effects this will have, and where it will lead you.

Students often mistake 'learn the rules first' to mean that they can never experiment or self-discover, and that they have no control over their education. This is generally the result of the sort of education they received as a young adult: 'do what you want' and 'anything goes' are principles that have become all too commonly and unthinkingly applied in many Western education systems. Such an approach will set up a student of magic for ultimate failure: they may learn some interesting things and feel more in control, but they will remain stuck on the first few rungs of the ladder of magic.

In magic as in ballet, if the basic and intermediate training is not solid and intelligent, then the advanced work will have no foundation to sit on. Proper magical training gives the magician not only knowledge and skill, but wisdom and safety. It allows the ancient patterns of magical dynamics to grow within the person so that they will have a good 'compass' for power and contact. Once the dynamics are learned properly, then the magician can apply their skills and knowledge to any magical or mystical system, and they can begin to experiment in a way that is rooted in *gnosis*. If you know that putting a 240 volt cable in your mouth is dangerous then you will not do that; but you will know what voltage is safe to work with, you will know that copper wires are good conductors of electricity and plastic wires are not, and you will use fuses in your experiments to stay safe as you explore how things work.

The training structure of Quareia works with the 'rules first' dynamic, and the basic structures and dynamics are laid out to give the student a flexible and intelligent basis for their magical knowledge. As the student progresses deeper into the course, more and more opportunities are presented for experimentation, tinkering, and invention. When something could be dangerous to them, such play is not encouraged. As an adept, once all the structures are learned, the student then understands why it was important to follow the rules and not break them. And with that knowledge and wisdom, they can plunge body and soul into magical experimentation in a way that is unique to them and their skills. That is the stage of magical evolution. That is the breaking of the rules in *gnosis*.

I am amazed at the number of students who want to play about with patterns, tools, and actions in the early stages of their training, usually on a whim or from something they have read in a book. They are doomed to stay on the apprentice rung of magic until they give up that approach. The basic system presented in the Apprentice section is there for a good reason, and unpicking and altering it will disengage the student from Quareia's magical pattern—and from its inherent protections. The current fashion of 'my ignorance is as good as your knowledge' cuts no ice in Quareia.

Of course, Quareia is set up in a way that people can do what they want with it, but if you truly wish to succeed in magic, then learn the rules first and gain a good level of competency. That is the way to evolve and develop as an intelligent magician.

What trips up early students, I think, is that they learn parts of a set system—Golden Dawn, Druidism, OTO, etc.—without realizing that the magic in that system is structure-specific and does not translate well into other forms of magic. Quareia does not work in that way. It builds and works from the structure that underpins all the different forms of magic. You learn the underlying patterns and fully understand them, then you can see for yourself how these other forms developed, why they developed, and what they are working with. Such an approach allows you to work magically with any other magical system in a coherent and intelligent way.

1.9   Conclusion

I hope this chapter has given you a basic overview of how the course was approached in its creation, and how its outer construction worked. Now that you know a bit about some of the dynamics and principles which underpin the course, you should have a better understanding of why the course is as it is, and how best to operate within it. This knowledge may be particularly important for students from Eastern cultures, as their approach to learning can be very different indeed, particularly with respect to the Mysteries. The rest of this book will look at more specific aspects of the Quareia training, common questions that have been asked, and ways to approach certain aspects of the training. With a course as vast as this one—it is similar in scope to a university degree—it is appropriate to offer guidance without disengaging the student from the basic steps, struggles, and decisions that they have to make for themselves.

Then the Lord God formed man of the dust of the ground, and breathed into his nostrils the breath of life; and man became a living soul.

And the Lord God planted a garden eastward, in Eden; and there He put the man whom He had formed.

And out of the ground made the Lord God to grow every tree that is pleasant to the sight, and good for food; the tree of life also in the midst of the garden, and the tree of the knowledge of good and evil.

And a river went out of Eden to water the garden; and from thence it was parted, and became four heads.

*And the Lord God took the man, and put him into the garden of Eden **to dress it and to keep it**.*

— Genesis 2:7, The Tanakh According to the Masoretic Text *and* JPS Hebrew/English Bible, *1917*

Chapter Two

Common Study Issues

If the doors of perception were cleansed everything would
appear to man as it is, infinite.

— *William Blake*

Subsequent chapters will deal with those aspects of the course about which students have been shown to need some in-depth advice and guidance. But in this chapter we will look at some general issues which have come to light, issues that I had not thought about or been aware of when I was writing the course.

2.1   Magic and modern life

There are a few aspects of modern life (and in various places around the world) that can clash with a magical path of study. Here we will look at the ones that seem to be causing the most problems for people.

2.2   Distraction and commercialism

The world has become a place of distractions. We are surrounded by constant noise and stimulation, and a lot of this stems from commercialism. Commercialism has its place and serves a necessary function, but in some countries it has become an overarching monster that infects everything it touches.

You cannot get away from it; and anyway to run from it would be counterproductive. You are in the age you are in, and must learn to function in whatever society you live in. The key is to make it work for you, not for you to work for it.

The neverending stream of media that pours from phones, televisions, and computers encourages people to be constantly plugged in to whatever devices are around them. New technology that makes things easier for you is exciting, particularly when you are young, but magicians have to be constantly aware of what is happening in their surroundings and why. Commercialism needs a consumer, and that is all you are to it: a person to be manipulated into buying things so that companies get your money and you get a dopamine hit from your acquisition.

This aggressive commercialism taps into an ancient human defence mechanism that we might call our 'inner squirrel.' A squirrel spends a lot of its time finding food and storing it for the winter. It gets *pleasure* out of this—a hit of dopamine squirted into its brain—and for a sound biological reason: its sense of satisfaction at keeping a full and ever-expanding larder ensures that it will survive the winter.

Our two most basic instincts are the same as the squirrel's: breed and store food. Those two root survival instincts are abused by advertising, which presents you with things that trigger either your breeding instinct or your instinct to store food. 'Sex sells.' 'More is better.' The more you buy, the better you feel, the safer and more in control you feel. But if you step back and realize this, then you can turn commercialism on its head and make it work *for* you.

The positive side of commercialism is that it makes a lot of useful things easily available. As a magician, it is very important that you spot and understand all the dynamics surrounding you in your modern life, so that you can engage with necessity rather than desire. The key to a lot of magic is simple necessity; but knowing what is necessary and what is not can be difficult for someone who has spent their life being marketed at all day, every day.

The biggest problem this sort of environment poses is its lack of silence. There is no downtime for the mind, and a constant unseen battle is being waged between your subconscious and the marketing machine. In such an environment it is difficult to get past the first few steps of a magical training, and this can prevent many sensitive people from ever progressing.

Let's treat this issue practically. The two main distractions are the TV and the smartphone. Both serve useful purposes and are now part of everyday life. But they can begin to rule your life and block you from magic if you are not careful. You have to learn to use them and be around them *as a magician*. There is a relatively recent notion that you can have it all, that you can keep enjoying all your consumption and your distractions and still be a true magical adept. That is not true. However, there are ways to balance things so that you can still enjoy the fruits of modern living while walking an ancient path. But you have to be careful and pay attention to your mind and everything around you.

2.3 Television

Many people keep a television going in their house day and night. They have it on as background noise during the day, as a source of entertainment at times, and as a companion as they sleep. This creates a constant background chatter in their home. Not only is this bad for magicians, but it is also bad for children.

Magic, development, and learning all need quiet times when your mind can wander and wonder. Quiet is also necessary when you need to focus. The needs of a magician are similar to those of a developing child. A child needs to have silent times when their imagination is the only thing that entertains them. Silent boredom is an important part of their development, for it is the breeding ground of the imagination, and the imagination is the key to magic.

My advice is not to have a television playing while you sleep, or while ever you are not actually sitting down and watching a program. Besides the constant noise it creates, passively letting all sorts of programs play in the background of your life can affect your mind and imagination: their content will settle deep in your imagination and can affect your inner vocabulary.

Your inner vocabulary is the language that inner beings/spirits will use to communicate with you. If it is passively and subconsciously picked up from reality TV shows, horror films, and god knows what else, then it can cause problems for inner contacts when you are trying to connect with them.

2.4   Smartphones

Smartphones can create similar problems. The instant and constant narrative available through social media can quickly become addictive. People constantly check their phones, and even take them to bed with them. They are often used as alarm clocks, but this can often slide into the person checking their phone if they wake up in the night; and they check it again the moment they wake up in the morning. This can cause creeping problems for a magician or magical student. Waking up in the middle of the night and having to lie quietly and think, is great exercise for your mind and imagination. It is also a time when the world around you is still and silent—hopefully—and this can allow deeper thoughts and analyses to surface.

This in turn affects how you dream and what you dream about. Dreaming for a magician is not only the brain processing its daily intake: it is also a time when the deeper spirit of the magician can get to work. A lot of magical work is done in dreams, and it is a time when warnings, communications and insights can surface. Anything that affects your dream state—television, phones, medications—can have a direct effect on your ability to dream deeply and magically.

So buy a simple alarm clock for the side of your bed, and keep your phone out of the bedroom. Learn to unplug and not be ruled by these devices that can deeply affect your mind in so many different ways.

I get many emails from young student magicians who have severe problems with meditation, stillness, and silence; the majority of them are plugged into devices day and night. Their minds have become trained to constant noise and input, so meditation and silence can be a real struggle.

It can be a good exercise to keep a tally for twenty-four hours of how many times you engage with a media device for passive noise, companionship, or entertainment. It can come as a bit of a shock to people to realize just how much of their day is spent connected to one media device or another.

Learn to use these devices to your advantage. A phone is primarily a source of *communication*. Be wary of allowing it to become your constant entertainer and companion. When you cease to use your smartphone passively, and start using it only for its real purposes such as communication and research, then at first you will go through a withdrawal and loneliness. But afterwards you will be driven to books, art, music, and your imagination. That is the fertile ground that breeds a strong magician.

Modern advances can be wonderful things, if you do not allow them to completely take you over. A good film or program can inspire you, uplift you, or inform you. Lying on the floor listening to a complex piece of music can fill you with emotion. Staring into the distance, deep in thought, is how great things are born. And leafing through books to find what you want gives you the opportunity to stumble across hidden gems, which a focused internet search does not. There is also the magical bonus that the book, as an object, can become a doorway. A computer cannot. Books and computers are different animals, and learning to work properly with both of them can really help you.

2.5 Sleep

Sleep is really important to magicians as it is when a lot of magical work happens: it is a time for learning, speaking, and communicating, and a time when spirits, deities, and inner contacts can get messages or warnings to you.

Currently, many magicians like to try to control their dreams to trigger lucid dreaming: this is simply fashion and nothing more. The more you try to control what happens in your sleep, the more you end up blocking real magical connection. So don't do it!

The length of sleep you get, and when you get sleep, are also both important. A lot depends on whether you are a night person or a day person, and whether your sleep patterns are dictated by work or, for instance, wanting to stay up late and play games. If you are a morning person then make sure you get to bed in plenty of time (I know, I am starting to sound like your mother), because the problems for magicians start to show when they do not get enough sleep. If your body and mind cannot get through their clearing-out process and still have to do their magical processing, then you will start to feel it.

In some countries there is competition between peers about how much work they can do and how little sleep they need. For a magician this is a lethal combination. Magicians need more sleep than most people, as they are processing more and often working or learning in their sleep.

Sometimes when I am doing a heavy round of magic, I need twelve hours sleep—nine at night and three during the day. I slept a great deal while writing the Quareia course, as I was processing so much contact and information. But normally, seven or eight hours a night is about average for a magician. Any less than that, and your health will likely start to suffer.

You should not sleep in a room with a television going. And the deeper you get into magic, the more you will have to watch what you have in the room where you sleep, as certain objects and images can have troublesome effects. This differs between magicians, but generally the deeper you get into magic, the more important it becomes to take care over your bedroom.

If you are the type of person that I call 'see through,' i.e. you have a thin inner skin and are easily affected by spirit contact, and find you are having troubled sleep, then sleeping with an eight-hour safe candle burning at night will help you. If it is too bright, then try putting it in a hanging sanctuary lamp or in a dish with tallish sides to block some of the light. Some of this is discussed in the course, so I do not need to go into it too much here.

Most importantly, get a good night's sleep. Don't watch movies just beforehand, as this can affect your inner narrative. If you are currently exploring a certain culture or mythos and you find an old film that connects with it, then that is an exception, as watching it just before you sleep help you tap into that stream of myth. But be warned, watching violent, aggressive, or badly unbalanced programs before you sleep will embed their narratives deeply into your subconscious, and this will affect your magical contact. Being a skilled magician means taking extra care of your mind, imagination, and emotions. They are the tools of your trade.

2.6 Time restraints

When the life of magic and the life of work clash heavily it can make for problems. Some people have two jobs and a family to support, and that can make magical study and practice difficult. If you have no spare time at all, it is best to wait for something to change before embarking on magical study.

However if you do have some spare time, but have time constraints, then being disciplined yet flexible will help a lot. For example, meditation. If you are not simply avoiding doing meditation, but really do not have twenty minutes to sit and meditate, then doing a few sessions of five minutes each, scattered throughout the day, will start the process off. I used to meditate on the bus to work, and when I had a lunch break I would eat, then find a quiet space to sit and meditate in silence for ten minutes.

When it comes to ritual acts, that can take up time, so plan ahead and manage your time properly. Once you have decided to do a ritual act and set a date, the process begins at that point. So if you set a date, stick to it.

If life is continually getting in the way of practising your magic, and it is not just that you want to watch a movie or play a game but you really are being blocked by your responsibilities, then you are probably being held back from magic for some reason. This happened to me a lot in my early days, and looking back, it saved my ass. I was too unstable and immature in my teens to be delving too deeply into magic, and the constraints of work and ballet kept me waiting for quite some time. I am a natural magician, and when that natural ability is mixed with the idiocy of youth, bad things can happen. The secret is to be honest with yourself and not make excuses, and to be serious and disciplined about your intent to study. Either do it and fully engage with it, or don't do it.

2.7 Family

Having children is another restraint on study, and you may have to put your studies on hold until your children are old enough. Magic does not happen in a bubble: it affects all aspects of your life and can also affect your children adversely. Each situation is different and you have to think carefully about what you plan to do and why. The magic in the Apprentice section is unlikely to harm any children you are connected to, but deeper study may.

The general rule is, do not do magic if you are a mother until your child reaches seven years of age. There are always differences unique to each individual, but in general, it is best to wait. I had to stop most of my magical practice when I had kids: I did not so much as pick up a tarot deck until my youngest was about two. I did not really start to resume my magical practice until my youngest was seven, and I have to say, it was the longest seven years of my life. But it was worth it. And in truth, you really don't lose all your magical connections: it is still around you, and beings will still connect with you, but any actual magical work should wait.

If you find that your child is magical—if they are clearly picking up on things and seeing things, then they may do very well around magic once they are about five, or you may find that magic affects them no matter how old they are. With such a child, the type of magic you do is important. Balanced magic rooted in the balanced Mysteries should not harm them, but they may need extra care and protection. Imbalanced or aggressive magic could affect them very badly indeed. When you take on the responsibility of having a child, as their mother, their wellbeing takes precedence over everything else. It does not matter how depressed or isolated it makes you feel, you have a responsibility to nurture and protect them above all else.

If you are a father, it can really vary as it depends upon your inner connection with your child. Some fathers have a deep inner connection with their children, regardless of how attentive or inattentive a parent they are in everyday life, and some do not. Your inner connection has nothing to do with being a good or bad father, it is simply either there or not. If you have a deep connection, then you have to wait until your child is old enough before you can continue your magical work. If you don't have a deep connection, then experiment with carefully continuing your studies, and watch closely how your child reacts. If you do some magical work and the child then starts having nightmares or getting sick, or seems to know what you have been doing, then they are being affected. If they seem just fine, then continue carefully, but remember that each magical act is an individual thing. Your child may be fine with some things and not with others.

The easiest way to find out if you have a deep inner connection with your child is to watch what happens to your inner energy when they are sick, injured, or disturbed. If your energy suddenly goes right down, but you are not ill and there is no other cause for your lack of energy, then it is likely that your inner energy is upholding them. In that case, you are deeply connected to them and you will have to be careful.

2.8   Resources

This can be a problem for people in some parts of the world. There are some things that the course states that you need, usually for a ritual, that can be hard to get. With things like cloths and candles, improvisation is good. Bed sheets can be cut up to make cloths. With candles, you do need a living flame when a candle is indicated, because the element of fire needs to be present, so an electric fake candle will not work. But tea lights can be used, as can small ghee or oil lamps that produce a flame. But be wary of oil that smells of paraffin, and of perfumed oil, and don't use scented candles. Certain scents, particularly synthetic ones, can close contact down. Inner contacts and spirit contacts can be sensitive to smells.

With recommended books, it is often only part of a book that you need, and often these books can be found online, as a lot of them are in the public domain. Some of the necessary texts are embedded into the course for you, and we will also be producing a collection of the classical texts you need so that you can get them cheaply. They will also be available as a free download.

If you cannot get oils, resins, and so forth, then work without them. It is usually a matter of do your best, use your imagination, and when there is something that is impossible to get, then work without it. Later, as a mentored student, if you really do need them, and cannot afford them, if we can, we will send them to you.

Once a student reaches the Initiate level of training and has been accepted for mentoring, if they cannot afford a Magicians' Deck then we will send them a free one. I also keep an eye out for secondhand books that are from the Quareia reading list, and when I find them cheaply, Quareia buys them to give for free to people who need them. In some countries even small amounts of money can be difficult to come by.

All these things are done for mentored students: they have demonstrated their ability to study the course by reaching Initiate level, and the mentoring shows commitment. If someone wants mentoring and they cannot afford to donate, it is done freely for them, and resources are given to them if they need it and we have what they need.

This is all done on an honour basis. Quareia is ruled by Ma'at, *balance*, and we take our responsibility to our students seriously.

We expect them to be truthful, and we give freely where there is real need. If someone decides to ask for freebies because they want to spend their money elsewhere, then the dynamic of Ma'at will kick in. It is a living magical power, and it will flow through the life of the student. It gives where there is need, and binds where there is untruthfulness. Two of the cornerstones of Quareia magic are honour and fellowship, and we will always make sure that any seeker genuinely walking the path of magical study has what is necessary for them.

We work closely with mentored students to make sure they are fully supported in their work, and as people help Quareia, we help students.

2.9 Ethics and culture

It has come to my notice that some countries' cultural and ethical concepts are so very different from those from which Quareia sprang that our students from those countries can easily become confused.

The stew that is Western magic was brewed in a cultural cauldron which stretched from the Eastern Mediterranean to the tip of Northwest Europe. The ancient Egyptians, Babylonians, Greeks, Romans, and Celtic tribes all added ingredients to that stew, as did many other peoples.

While countries like India have much in their ancient history and culture that is similar to that which produced Western magic, once you move further east into countries like China and Vietnam, the common language of magical reference points changes. Also, where countries have been Communist for some time there can be some difficulty in understanding the basics of magical thought. In an atheist society, it is difficult for someone to think about deities and so forth.

For example, in a conversation with a student from China, I tied myself in knots trying to explain the power dynamics of the Tree of Life. When a person has no cultural concept of Divinity, things start to get complicated.

I have no idea what the solution to this is. The only advice I can give to someone studying the Quareia course from a radically different culture is to go into the course with an open mind, and deal with each step as you come to it. Don't try to analyse ahead, as you will only get more and more confused. Learn what is directly in front of you, and as things start to trigger and work, then inner contacts will draw close and help guide you. Think of it as learning a whole new language. Don't try to read and understand the highest level of literature at the beginning: learn the baby steps, one at a time, and you will get there.

I think what will happen is that people who come to Quareia from different cultural backgrounds will study it in their own way, and out of that, as they complete the course, a whole new genre of magic will develop. Once a student has the actual magical vocabulary and has adapted some ways of magical working to their own cultural context, then their magic will evolve down a whole new road that is perfect for them. Also it will trigger the inner contacts, spirits, and powers of their land, and it will start to take on a life of its own. It will still be the same magic, just with a different accent.

In practical terms, I would also say that you should adapt and be flexible. Don't worry about not fully understanding something, particularly in the early days of your training. Often in magic the understanding catches up with you when you are ready.

2.10 Myths

At various points in the course, students are given small sections of particular mythologies to look at, read, and discover what is going on magically under the surface. It is important to study Egyptian, Roman, and Greek myths carefully, as they contain many hidden dynamics that need to be understood.

However, there are also points in the course where students are given various Northern European mythologies to look at and analyse. If you are from a radically culture and you cannot make sense of these European myths, then find a similar ancient myth with the same theme,—not a modern work of fiction—from your culture and use that instead. To do this, look at the techniques used to analyse the myth, and at the general subject matter, for example sleeping kings and queens, or warriors who are said to not be dead but sleeping in a cave or hill, and who will emerge when the nation is under threat. Similar stories can be found in the Far East, but where there has been Communist suppression of myths and stories you may have to work hard to find what you are looking for. Old songs and old children's stories can often be good places for a culture's mythology to hide.

Once you move beyond the surface of magic, you will find that the deeper undercurrents and dynamics are the same in every culture, as they are inherent to humanity; as such, a culture's myths and stories often hide these deeper undercurrents.

The key is to look at how the myth is approached in the lesson, what tasks are given, and what the lesson is trying to teach you. Once you understand the approach being used, you can use that approach on a myth from anywhere: you are learning how to learn.

2.11   Fear

This is a major stumbling block for a lot of students, and an issue that had not occurred to me. We live in a time of conspiracies, media propaganda, and social manipulation; untruths, fantasies, and bullshit ideas all flourish in our social media, news, and entertainment.

As the education systems of some Western countries degenerate, more and more people cannot tell the difference between fantasy and reality or fiction and non-fiction, and they believe anyone who speaks with authority, even if they are talking total nonsense.

This is a particular problem in magic, as one of the main tools of the magician is their mind. The mind and the imagination are regulated by hormones to some extent, and when a person is kept constantly in a state of fear it begins to affect how they think and imagine. This sets up a pattern of behaviour that becomes the norm, of being constantly in a low level of fear and stress.

Not being able to trust the media narrative, yet lacking discernment themselves, some students—particularly younger students who have grown up in this odd environment—develop an outlook on the world in which everything is perceived as a threat.

Inner contacts, spirits, beings, and deities are all perceived, consciously and subconsciously, as threats. So you have a young student with a deep desire to study magic and mysticism, but who is also terrified of everything that goes bump in the night. (This can be particularly exacerbated by watching a lot of violent horror movies, which often weave aspects of the occult into their narratives.)

I have had many emails from distraught individuals terrified out of their minds because a spirit tried to interact with them, or because the door creaks too much, or because they think demons will attack them and eat their eyeballs (I shit you not).

Healthy caution in magic is one thing; adopting the narrative of the violent American horror movie genre as your inner vocabulary and magical narrative is quite another, and it is not healthy.

I am at a loss as to how to remedy this issue, and can only suggest that people take greater care over what they expose their imaginations to. If you do feel something is happening to you, and some of it is similar to something in the movies, then it is likely that either your mind is playing tricks on you, or you are interpreting a genuine attempt at contact as something hostile.

There are magical protections woven into the course's structure to protect you from unnecessary bad experiences: if you are following it as prescribed, then you are safe. Just learn to interpret what is happening around you. Common sense is always the reference point when you are not sure what is going on.

And when a magical 'expert' touts a horror narrative, know that they are not an expert; they are an unethical person who is either mad, bad, or stupid. Usually what lies behind such behaviour is a wish for authority—pedestal standing—or money. Ego and money are always the bedfellows of such behaviour.

2.12   Dead Ends

This can become a serious problem for students, and being trapped in a dead end of study will likely block you from reaching deeper into magic. The dynamic of the *dead end* is an inherent part of the study of magic: its purpose is to unravel out of the magical arena those who are unsuited, mentally or physically, for it.

However, it is also a dynamic that suitable students can get stuck in if they are not careful. Students stuck in dead ends stay in their comfort zone, or focus on one aspect of the training alone, or repeatedly go back to an earlier lesson and try to perfect it. All these things stop students moving forward and developing, and instead keep them trapped in a loop of repetition.

Some get trapped in the tarot dead end, doing lots of readings, and reading as many books as they can find on the subject, instead of simply doing the step they were assigned to take in a lesson and thus securing a building block for their path ahead. Instead of securing that building block, the student delves into the depths of tarot, trying to learn everything they can about it. But tarot is not truly learned that way. It is learned by practice *alongside other magical practices*. You are like a juggler keeping plates spinning: you have to pay attention to all your plates equally, not focus on one in particular.

It is the same with astrology and ritual: these are things that people feel they can learn a lot about simply by reading and playing at it a little bit. But by not paying attention to the other aspects of their training, they miss how the powers are interwoven, and end up locked out of the system.

In later chapters we will look at the dead ends found in each of the foundation core skills that can particularly trap and hold the unsuspecting student. Often a student will rationalize their dead end by saying they want to get something exactly right before moving on. Magical training really does not work like that. If the student cannot trust the course's steps to take them where they need to go, then they will find themselves unable to penetrate the evolving aspects of the training. This course needs to be studied in small but frequent steps, not by crash studying one particular aspect.

The other general dead end that will unravel a student out of training is becoming an instant expert who seeks to lecture everyone in their magical group of friends, taking on the mantle of authority before they have even got past a few beginner modules. This is an example of the *messiah trap*, an ancient trap in magic in which an immature ego is glamoured into becoming a saviour or expert when they know nothing and cannot help themselves, let alone others.

It is also a symptom of projection. When a person cannot cope with something, they rally to others who also cannot cope and set themselves up as saviours. This gives them a little circle of acolytes, but it locks them out of the training. A person who gets stuck in this dynamic cannot begin to move forward in gnosis, as they have no self-awareness.

When you first learn a skill, it is understandable to want to use it to help others; but a student must know *why* they want to do that. Do they really want to help others, or do they want some modicum of authority?

2.13   Hitting a wall

This is the most common issue of all, and it is inherent in all forms of classical training. Intense long-term study has its own tides, and this is particularly true of magical training. There are times in the training when you will hit an energetic wall. You cannot seem to make progress, you are exhausted and demoralized, and you feel like a failure. You are not. Not at all. It is a good sign, though a painful one.

There are various reasons why this happens. One is that it is normal with any intense training to hit such a wall: it is part of the process. And with magical training, there can be an awful lot happening in the world to cause inner 'bad weather' which will either pull you into action in your sleep, or lock you out for your safety. If you are pulled into working in your sleep, then all your magical energy will be used up with such work, leaving you with nothing for practice. And if you are locked out, then no matter what you try to do you will not be able to access any sense of magically 'moving forward.'

If you are hitting the wall constantly and do not feel that you are moving forward at all, then put your current lesson on pause, and move on with the course. Come back to the stuck bit when you are ready. We do not all develop the same way, and magic tends not to work in straight lines. The course's step-by-step training is important for its overall coherence, for anchoring the foundation, and for developing a proper sense of training. Its steps will be in the right order for ninety percent of its students. However, ten percent always develop in a different way. Do not use this as an excuse to skip forward if you are just bored or feel that a lesson is beneath you: a lot is hidden in even the easiest of the lessons. However, if you are seriously hitting the wall... then move on. Just don't forget to come back soon and finish off the stuck lesson.

If you are finding that you are stuck *and* exhausted all the time, then one of two things (or both) is happening. Either you are working in your sleep, or you are being stretched.

Working in your sleep happens naturally with a lot of students without them realizing. Having lots of weird dreams and broken sleep? This is a symptom of your deeper self having taken over and started working in your sleep. A lot of the work in Quareia is about service, and sometimes you can get drawn into service work in your sleep, particularly when the situation is critical. At the moment the Western world is struggling with a dangerous buffoon of a leader with his finger on the nuclear trigger, and with the rise of fascism in various parts of the world. This situation can develop into a nasty long-term scenario for the whole planet, so it is no wonder that people are working hard in their sleep.

It is important to recognize this when it happens. If your tarot skills have developed enough, then do a reading to see what is happening in your sleep. It will likely show work, conflict, or struggle. Whenever you are working in your sleep, you must make sure that you are not overworking magically in your waking life. So don't overdo the training work: take some time out. Be mundane. It is important to learn to manage your energy, and to recognize when you have been working in your sleep without realizing it.

Being stretched is a more difficult thing to explain. It is akin to being rearranged, and it often happens to people on magical or mystical paths. Again, you will feel blocked and tired. When that happens, rest, slow your magical work down (but don't stop), and be as normal as possible. You will feel when the stretching is over, as your energy will come rushing back in.

If you have exhaustion and *physical* symptoms, then go see a doctor to make sure you are not ill.

For the most part, hitting a wall means that you are backing up in preparation for a major leap forward. You will be blocked from moving forward properly until everything is in place around you, and you have processed internally what you have already learned. The key to hitting walls is to wait patiently. Continue your basic practice, and don't overdo it or push yourself. View it as treading water while you wait for the sluice gates to open. When the timing is right, everything will suddenly leap forward, and you will be back in the fast lane.

Remember, real magical training is not a short one or two year jaunt. It is a long marathon. There will be times for sprinting, times for resting, and times for time out. Find your pace and your limits, and don't ever feel you have failed because you get stuck... that is just bullshit. We all get stuck, we all take time out. I still do, after decades of magic. It is called being human.

2.14 Cherry picking

Cherry picking happens when a student not only looks ahead at the more advanced modules (which is not a problem in itself) but decides that there are elements of the course that are beneath them, so they skip them and instead dive into the more advanced work that has grabbed their attention.

There are various problems with this approach, and the student often ends up getting damaged, or getting the attention of hostile beings. I get endless emails from terrified student magicians who are being hounded and who have made themselves ill through their actions.

The roots of this problem are not trusting the structure of the course and not taking the work seriously enough. Ego can also be a factor: the student feels, because they have done some previous study, that it is okay for them to pick and choose.

One of the overarching problems in magical training and study today is a lack of foundation skills: if those are not rock solid, then the whole 'house' of a person's magic is built on sand. Everything is fine until real power or real contact happens, and then everything goes down the toilet and the student is in a mess.

To be honest, I am not willing to clean someone up and put them back on their feet if they have harmed themselves by ignoring advice. That might sound harsh, but I don't have the time it takes to help such people, and learning from your bad experiences is either a really good teacher or a really good filter: you either drop out of the course, or you learn to sort yourself out. All the skills you need to help yourself in such situations are outlined in the very first Apprentice module. You either apply them and learn a harsh lesson, and thus mature a bit so that you can study properly, or you drop off the magical path: you are filtered out. Magic takes no prisoners, and the earlier a student realizes that and takes their study seriously, the better.

This course is built in layers. Each layer has aspects of protection, strengthening, and knowledge acquisition. If you miss a vital part of a layer, then you will likely have a serious weakness in your magic. Everything stands on what was done before. This course is built like a pyramid with a wide, solid base, and as the pyramid rises, the structure becomes more condensed and complex. When you look at a pyramid from the outside, you do not see the internal architecture that distributes stress and upholds everything. So it is with Quareia.

If you are curious and wish to look ahead in the course, then do so. But keep in mind that what you read is not the same as what you experience when you actually do the work. Do not be fooled into thinking that because you have read something, you fully understand it. This is not a theoretical course alone. All the theory has its root in the direct experience which constitutes seventy percent of the learning. Most students will walk the path a lesson at a time. A few will be prompted to engage in a practical lesson a step or two ahead, usually for a specific reason. Do not do that unless you get a serious prompt, and you must also still continue with the given sequence of lessons and *redo* the more advanced step when you get to it. Needing to do a lesson early is rare: do not let your curiosity or your whims be a reason for doing so. Magic sometimes has its own timing, but the steps must also be done in sequence to make sure that all aspects of the pattern, the protections, and the learning are in place.

2.15 Broken links

I have mentioned this earlier in this guide, and I have to apologize for putting internet links in the course. They vanish so quickly. None of them are critical: they are just there to make your research easier by giving you somewhere to start. Use a search engine when you come across broken links: you will certainly find something useful, and even if you do not find what we were trying to show you, it will not affect your training in any way.

I learned a lot of harsh lessons from writing the apprentice section, and I had to smarten up with how I approached things to make sure that the course and the information in it would last in the long term.

A final note: the internet is becoming increasingly commercialized, locked down, and threatened. It would be worthwhile for any serious student of Quareia to download and store, or even print out, the whole course. The course is also available in book form: the cheapest form is the three large paperbacks, one for each section. We have produced them as cheaply as possible to make sure that as many people as possible can access them, and they should also be available in UK and USA libraries on request.

Various people around the world are also working on translating the course into different languages, and these translations will also be distributed in as many ways as possible to help people access Quareia.

I am striving to give back the Divine in myself to the Divine in the All.

— *Plotinus*

Chapter Three

Approaching Magical Study

The seeker is as a cracked vessel. Through direct experience, the cracks are filled first with copper, then with silver, and finally gold. Then, and only then, the vessel can hold the Water of Life.

In this chapter we will look at general advice, and some general pitfalls that a student can tumble into. I hope it will give you the advice you need to be clear about how you are going to approach your magical training.

3.1 Discipline

The first and most important skill to acquire if you wish to train seriously in magic is discipline. For some this comes naturally, for many it is a struggle, and for some it can become a barrier: too much discipline and you end up locking yourself down by obsessing over achievements and goals; too little and you are left floundering around the edges of magic.

The first step towards developing a healthy discipline is to see it as a method of approach that gets you where you wish to go. Some people can become obsessive about discipline, so that without noticing the discipline itself becomes their goal. This sets the student up to 'fight' the course, which will result in them constantly hitting walls they cannot get beyond.

A healthy approach to developing discipline is to approach the course within the rule of absolutes: work on what is in front of you, enjoy it, and explore it, without constantly looking for a long-lost horizon. Once you have the right mindset—that your goal is to achieve what is before you—then you can develop a routine that will take you to that goal.

In addition, be adaptable. Everyone is different, and you should know yourself better than anyone. Don't fool yourself, but also listen to your internal voice. Magic never works like clockwork, and it ignores schedules. It ebbs and flows like a river, so learn to ebb and flow with its power. At times it is right to break your discipline, for inner or outer reasons, and other times you have to keep going with your practice even when you don't feel like it. The key is learning, by direct experience, how to have a constant relationship with magic and its practice.

Manage your time properly. Be pragmatic when you need to be. Remember, it is a long marathon, not a sprint. When you fail, pick yourself up, dust yourself off, and get walking the path again. Many failures on the way are inevitable, and you will learn as much from them as you will from your successes. The key to overall success is to enjoy the path, be challenged, learn, evolve, and grow; not to beat yourself up and sulk in the corner.

Set your study and practice schedules for a month and no longer; and sort out your meditation routine on a week-by-week basis. This allows for flexibility. Life sometimes throws curve balls at you, so being flexible will help.

Setting your meditation schedule for just a week at a time particularly allows you a lot of flexibility, as life is always changing. If you get locked in a routine that is too tight and too rigid, then either you will end up failing, or you will find yourself becoming dependant on your unchanging meditation schedule. Flexibility is always the key.

Also, for those of you who have problems with discipline generally or meditation specifically, setting a small, achievable goal for yourselves each week will greatly benefit you. Achievement makes you want to do more; failure can make you want to give up. So don't set yourself up for failure. And if you have a bad week and everything goes to shit, then simply write that week off and be fresh and ready for the following week.

3.2 Study approach

Do not approach the course as if you are cramming for exams. You are not. You are on an adventure. Let curiosity drive you, not ambition to be top of the class: there *is* no top of the class in Quareia. Each magician who becomes an adept through Quareia will be truly unique. Real, powerful magic creates individuals, which is why this is mostly a lone path. It does not create hierarchies, perfect students, or super groups: these are all things we wish for as a result of a subconscious search for power and status. That is not magic, that is misplaced ego.

Magical training is very much about having experiences that are subsequently informed by knowledge. Those experiences are then built on through repeated work, practice, and applying your new skills to the world around you. To flourish on such a path, take your time, enjoy the journey, and let the journey become your life.

One important point: follow the lessons exactly. Do not be tempted to change aspects of the work, as this will lock you out of the system. Everything in the lessons is there for a specific magical reason. I have come across students who want to change the directional pattern to suit their perspective, or to change the use of the tools, use a different tarot deck, or approach ritual or vision in a different way. This will set you up for failure, as you are working inside a coherent pattern. Change the pattern, and the whole structure will disengage.

In practical terms, there are some things that frequently trip up magical students in their study approach. Remember, this is not a degree course where simply doing lots of reading will get you where you want to go; it is a practical, skills-based course that is informed by reading.

Let us have a look at some of the things that can trip you up in your studies or cause you difficulties. Some of these have to do with how you approach your study, and others are dynamics that will trip you up if you are not careful. Because Quareia is not a theoretical course, a lot of the things that can derail you are not directly related to your study, but are practical dynamics to do with how you approach the magic, the material world, and yourself.

3.3   Confirmation bias

Confirmation bias can become a net that will easily entangle you due to the nature of magical study and the personal and psychological barriers we erect around us. It is something that in truth, you can never quite get away from. Magic uses our imagination, and our imaginations are informed by many things: our culture, experiences, likes, dislikes, and so forth. Survival mechanisms use patterns of recognition: we gravitate to what we recognize and we build upon that. As we build, we sort through our 'building materials' and take what we know fits, and we discard what doesn't.

This mechanism serves many purposes for us, but it can also hobble our learning and evolution: we can end up in an echo chamber of what we recognize, rejecting what does not fit. It is the same mechanism that discourages a child from trying new foods: they stay with familiarity unless there is peer pressure to try something different. The same mechanism also drives fundamentalism, and it can seriously warp our mental model of the world.

A lot of magical understanding comes from seeing, recognizing, and working with patterns, whether these are patterns of behaviour, patterns of energy, patterns of mythos, or patterns of words. Normal magical development means seeing a pattern in something, *not noticing* the bits that do not fit, and coming to conclusions that form the magical action. This is a normal developmental process in one's personal magical evolution. The problems occur when the magician sees a pattern, *notices* parts that do not fit, and then *ignores them*. Any subsequent work that relies on that 'ignoring' will set up a path of devolution within the magician. This is the trap of the negative application of confirmation bias. It is also an important deep dynamic of mystical magic: not knowing, and acting from innocence is harmless. Knowing, and acting regardless of the 'knowing', by ignoring what you know, creates a power imbalance that quickly spins out of control.

3.4   Messiah trap

I speak a lot about this and repeat myself many times. This is not to annoy you, but because it is so important to be aware of it, as it is the biggest trap for all magicians at every level of competence. I spoke earlier in this book about this dynamic as a surface presentation, but the deadlier form is its deeper presentation, which works through the pattern recognition mechanisms of our consciousness.

When you read Classical, ancient, and mythic texts, on one level you are looking at the cultural and mythological aspects of a people. However, many of those texts also have a deeper layer that speaks to initiates of the Mysteries. Embedded within the texts are dynamics that tell of stages of mystical and magical development, and these layers appear in ancient Egyptian, Classical, and ancient Greek texts. They also appear in Jewish, Christian, and

Islamic texts, with the dynamic attached to the prophets of these religions.

These dynamics also appear in magical visionary work, though for the most part they are not written about in magical texts. For the volumes of magical inner work in the Quareia course, a large percentage is left unsaid. These are the parts of magical work that must be found by the magician alone; when they are experienced, mentors and teachers know that their student is developing well and connecting with the deeper inner patterns of magic.

These deeper experiences come in dreams and visions, and occasionally in outer encounters in the world. The only way I can describe them is to say that they are inner narratives and experiences that any true magician on the path of development will experience in some form or another. Their presentation can vary from person to person, but their underlying patterns are the same.

When someone is thrust into one of these experiences, it can be intense and profoundly life changing. If the magician is grounded, is rooted in the pattern of their work, and has a good foundation under them, then the experience can show them the reality of the path they are walking, where it is going, or who they are at the deepest level: it is a pure revelation. It is something that has been recorded from ancient times: it is hidden in texts, and once you have experienced it then you will spot it lurking in the corner of an epic tale, or in a religious recitation. It is a shining light that truly awakens your spirit to your eternal self and to your communion with everything around you.

If someone is not properly prepared, through lack of training or through not adhering to it, or if they are not grounded and disciplined, and they still manage to trigger one of these experiences, then it can tip them over the edge into mental illness.

Remember the quote at the top of this chapter about the cracked vessel? The messiah trap blows the cracked vessel wide open, spilling its contents, rather than healing the cracks.

In the apprentice section, this can rear its head in the weakest way by tempting the student to become a pedestal stander, as is explained in the previous chapter. If the student spots their ego trip and remedies the problem, then their vessel will be strengthened and prepared for the bigger exposure to that power later. A lot of magical training contains innate 'traps' in which weaknesses in the personality/ego are brought to the surface so that they can be recognized and dissolved. The work itself helps in that process: that is the layer of copper.

This is why it is so important to follow a classical training properly, and not jump about or dabble within it. The Apprentice and Initiate parts of the course are designed to close up your vessel's cracks gradually and strengthen it so that it is ready for such an experience.

So what happens when it all goes badly wrong? If the lessons in the Apprentice section are not learned or are ignored, then any creeping or deeply hidden wish to 'save the world' or be a 'prophet' will rapidly surface when the student has a powerful experience.

The student may have a strong visionary experience which can at times mirror the narrative of a Biblical or religious figure such as a prophet or messiah. This is because those narratives have their roots within the ancient Mysteries: these experiences are hallmarks of deep inner connection and soul evolution. Having one does not mean you are a messiah; it is simply you making a profound connection with Divinity and the Mysteries that transcends religion and culture.

When the student or magician is not fully grounded, having such an experience can trigger the feeling that the magician is a saviour, a Divine being of some sort, or a messiah (in Christian cultures). As soon as the magician takes that unbalanced narrative for the truth, they will begin to spin out of control. Obsession moves in, as does mental imbalance, and their resulting behaviour can mirror forms of fundamentalism.

This tends to happen in magicians with a mental health weakness or an imbalance of some sort—usually something minor or in remission. People with more serious mental health issues tend not to get far enough into magic for such experiences to trigger, though it does occasionally happen. When a person takes on contacted classical magical training and follows it properly, then the powers and contacts within it will slow the student down enough in their studies to make sure that their inner 'muscle' is slowly strengthened. Through this, they learn to work with any inherent issues to stabilize and build foundations. In such cases, any imbalance triggered by these experiences will be minor, and will be recovered from quickly enough.

But when that development process is circumvented, and the filters skipped over, then it can seriously unravel the student out of magic for that lifetime. They become vocal messiahs of a path, declaring or at least hinting at their own godhood, and the final result is a total mental breakdown from which they often never recover.

I have had to witness this many times with potentially brilliant magicians who felt that their natural ability excluded them from the need for long-term serious training. It is sad to see and so unnecessary: so please take heed of this warning.

As an aside, when you do read classical or ancient texts and you recognize some of your experiences within them, remember that the overall message to take from this is that you have had a powerful experience that shows you are treading in the footsteps of the many who have walked the path before you. You are not special; you are finally *awake*.

3.5 Narrowed attention

One of the common mistakes that people make in long, in-depth training is to let their perceptions and attention get narrow when they are studying. This is a normal mechanism that triggers with any specialized training, and in some subjects it can be useful: the more you focus on one aspect of a subject, the more you can get out of it—but the less you see peripheral details.

This enables, for example, a scientist to look in great detail at an aspect of their specialization and spot things that an untrained person could never see. This is also important in magic, but here it is equally important not to miss the periphery, as often that is where magic leaves a trail of crumbs for you to follow.

It can be difficult to maintain adequate focus while also keeping enough of an eye out for information, contact, discovery, and development on the periphery. Magic flows through everything in life, and can speak to you out of many places. Because of this, the course is designed not only to teach you focus, but also to teach you to look outside of those areas which you perceive as magical. You will study many different things that are not directly related to magic, not only for the richness of experience and knowledge you can gain from them, but also to teach you how to find precious gems of magic in seemingly non-magical subjects.

If you stay aware of these two opposing dynamics of focus and peripheral attention, and keep a wide view of your surroundings while you focus carefully on the topic at hand, then you will do just fine. Magical focus on a specific thing will often trigger a response in a completely different area of your life: so pay attention, and you will harvest everything that you need to evolve and grow.

3.6   Not everything is magical

Many seemingly mundane things can happen as a result of magic, as it seeps throughout everything it touches and affects everything. However, it is easy to start thinking that everything that happens to you is magical: this is another trap. One of the skills a student magician must learn is how to discern what has been triggered by magic and what has not.

This becomes an issue when a student starts to believe that every time something negative happens it was caused by magic. Sometimes, shit happens. It can be that simple: it just is what it is. The skill of discernment is a mixture of practical experience, common sense, and divination when necessary. It is not easy, but it is an important skill to master. Thinking that everything is caused by magic means the student ends up not taking responsibility for themselves, and becomes a victim of life. But thinking that *nothing* is caused by magic stops the magician from developing, as often the magical kick-backs that affect your life can teach you a great deal.

It is about finding a healthy middle ground. I usually start by assuming that something has a mundane cause, but I will then look deeper just to check. Each experience you have can teach you something, so that you gradually build a vocabulary of 'effects' until eventually you learn to spot the hallmarks of magic. But even now I do not presume that an effect is magical: I always check, particularly when action may be needed.

3.7 Loss aversion

This can be a tough one, particularly in a consumer society. Magic triggers necessary change, and this is part of your growth and evolution as a magical student. Often the necessary change is to let go of something that you are clinging to.

In the Apprentice part of the course, there are exercises and actions that help trigger the skill of letting go. It really is a skill, and something that needs to be fostered and strengthened within you if you are to step forwards into adept magic.

People cling to belongings, ideas, people, places, etc. When those things (or some of those things) no longer have a place or purpose in your life, they can act as bindings or traps that hold you back from evolving. One of the first things that can happen, when you first make inner contact, is that the contact may spot something you are clinging to that is detrimental to you, and will ask you to relinquish it. If you resist then the inner contact will withdraw, for if you cannot let go of something that is creating an imbalance within you, then you cannot handle power.

And that is the root of the dynamic: learning how to let go of things teaches you how to handle real power when it is necessary. If you are lent magical power for some necessary purpose and you then cling to that power, it will begin to unravel you—and ultimately it will destroy you.

This can be a difficult dynamic to understand when you are in a culture that judges you by your belongings and by how much you consume. That mentality seeps into relationships, creates obsessions, and locks people down into the trap of accumulation.

Learning to let go when asked, and when you realize that something is not necessary, it allows old, outworn patterns in your life to be shed. This makes room for what is necessary to come into your life. The key point, which many magicians do not understand, is that when you walk through life without clinging to things, people, or places, but instead walk a path of necessity, then when you lack what you need, it is given to you. Making sure that your path is clear of unnecessary clutter—physical clutter, emotional clutter, whatever—allows power triggered by inner contacts to flow through your life pattern so that you get whatever it is that you need.

It will flow through mundane channels: money, shoes, a car, a partner, an area to live in. Of course these things do not fall from the clouds and magically land at your feet; rather you are put in the right place at the right time to make sure that what you need flows to you through mundane channels. The deeper you go in magic and magical service, the stronger this dynamic becomes. But first the cupboards must be emptied and cleaned, and your attachments shed, before this dynamic can begin to trigger. Once you stop clinging and let go, then power can start to flow.

In the early Apprentice modules, this understanding and dynamic is triggered both by simple ritual—in which you learn to give/output before you take/input—and by some practical work in which you sort out your living space and belongings. It starts in the mundane world, and as you step deeper into the training different layers emerge, so that this process becomes ever more powerful and more profound. So if you have an ingrained aversion to loss, then you should start working on it now. Give away things that you like but do not need: pass them down the line to those who need them.

3.8   Mythic reading and psychologizing

This is a major stumbling block for magicians when they look at ancient, classical, and mythological texts: they read them through a psychological filter. People are taught to think that ancient mythic texts were intended as stories to alter people's behaviour or to get them to search within themselves for answers to life's problems.

Myths can indeed be used that way, and with a few of them that is indeed their main function. However, they are the minority: a large portion of mythic and ancient texts are really about *regional power dynamics*, and when read through a magical lens, their deeper layers of meaning surface.

They served, and still do serve, as guides: they tell you the inner power dynamics behind the presentation of something, and they often explain how to deal with specific regional magical issues and supply the correct keys for doing so. The issues they tackle are often those caused by clashes between humans and land beings or deities: the myths tell you what to do about them, and what *not* to do. If you are magically trained then you can spot the references to tools, methods, and actions. One of the skills of the magician is to read such texts, extract the necessary information, and put it into action.

Myths are a good example of how magic hides in plain sight. To the mundane reader, a myth is an exciting and interesting tale which often contains general advice for living. But beneath that layer hides magic for those with the keys to unlock it; this was a way of passing magical information down through the generations.

The habit of approaching myths through a psychological lens distances the student from real magical learning. It also belittles the knowledge and skill of those who wrote such texts. This is glaringly apparent when we look at ancient Egyptian texts. Such texts appear simplistic, but they are not—not by any stretch of the imagination. They contain layer after layer of magic and magical advice, and for the magician who has been trained to look at them properly, they are endless source of magical knowledge, wisdom, and instruction; and this is true for both the living and the dead.

This way of looking at myth is taught throughout the course. If you start by completely dropping the psychological approach to ancient and Classical mythic texts, then you will slowly begin to see all the other layers of communication hidden in them.

3.9 Discernment

The skills of sound judgement and discernment also need plenty of healthy development if you are going to become a magician. And discernment is one of the hardest skills to learn when you are confronted by a subject matter you know little or nothing about.

In the last few decades, magic has fairly burst into the public consciousness and into popular culture. More and more people have become interested in it, in various ways and for various reasons. Wherever there is an audience, there will be someone looking to sell product to them. Often the person doing selling the product has little real knowledge and is basically full of shit.

The result is students being overwhelmed by lots of different aspects of magic, some that have their roots in truth and some that have their roots in fantasy. The confusion has been compounded by movies and games: they become the narrative in the mind of the student, and this locks them out of real magic. The fake glamour takes precedence. Remember, not everything you see in a 'historical' movie is real, not every monster or demon on TV is real, and not everything you read on the internet is real.

A healthy bullshit detector is a good thing to develop, and that is done slowly and painfully by experience, study, and by staying objective. Sometimes it can be difficult to discern the truth from the make-believe, as real magic is often far weirder than fiction; but it is also rooted in common sense. One good general rule is that if someone is making huge sums of money from something 'magical,' then for the most part they will be selling bullshit with a few grains of truth mixed in.

3.10 Tides and timings

These catch out a lot of magicians, even adepts, so being aware of them from the beginning of your training will be helpful. Dealing with tides and timings is not something to obsess over or overthink; just be aware of them and keep them in the back of your mind.

We are surrounded by inner tides of energy and power all the time. They ebb and flow like the seasons, but often without the same predictability. These are inner tides of nature, and are usually creative or destructive: they are something you will learn a lot about in the course.

Magic has its own tides, as does your fate, your body energy, and so forth. We exist within a complex dance of powers and energies. When you engage in magical training, you become more aware of these tides, and that also magic has its own timing. As an apprentice you will likely not spot tides much, but you will slowly develop a feel for them and how they affect you.

As an apprentice, if you are flexible with your approach, you will notice that at times energy comes in and fills you, and at other times the tide goes out and you are left feeling tired and drained. There are lots of other reasons for such feelings, but you will slowly start to distinguish between these and when they come from some magical act or from an 'inner weather' tide. Once you engage with magical training, you develop more of a sensitivity to things, and you also become more visible to such tides: they affect a magician where they would not necessarily affect a mundane person.

This dynamic is too complex to go into here, and it is covered throughout the course in different ways. But some general good advice for you at this stage is *learn to bend with the wind so that you do not break in a storm*. Pace yourself, adapt when necessary, and rest when necessary. And go undercover—be mundane, do no magic, no readings, etc—when you get the feeling that something threatening is looming.

Discernment is key here: are you just tired because you stayed up late or drank too much? Are you bored, grumpy, or coming down with a minor sickness? Or has a strange, unpleasant feeling, or a feeling of being drained, suddenly come upon you for no reason? If so, then it may be a tide affecting you. (There are other magical reasons for feeling like that, but they should not generally affect an apprentice.) This is where being truthful to yourself is important, and how you learn to discern between the different things that could be affecting you.

3.11   Emotions in magic

This is a major stumbling block for apprentices, for a variety of reasons. As you progress through the course and have various encounters and experiences, you will learn firsthand why emotions can be such a problem in magic. But as emotions can also affect your early studies, I will briefly address them here.

Quareia stretches in many directions of magic and looks at many different approaches to magic, so it is very likely that some students will trip up with the use of emotion at some point.

A new student with mystical leanings will likely bring into their practice Divine adoration, and/or the search for 'bliss.' This is purely the result of cultural and religious programming that has developed over thousands of years. Divine adoration and bliss are in fact deeply misunderstood terms, particularly in the West, and as we live in an emotive society, it is easy to bring a sort of emotive searching into our magical practice.

It is very important that you realize that when you are an apprentice, you have little experience with inner beings, and will be easily fooled. Certain types of beings are profoundly parasitical, and the food they seek is emotion, or the energy given off by emotions. These beings can manipulate your mind and practice to get you to have an emotional experience. You adore the being, the being says, 'thank you very much,' and it sucks up all your energy and leaves.

As a student develops into adepthood, they will begin to realize that there is a path in magic that opens an interface between themselves and the Divine, but no emotions are involved. The depth of the experience goes beyond the chemical emotions of the body, and reaches deep into their soul/spirit. It is a profound experience and changes you forever. But to get there, the magician needs to learn that deep connections that can be made that do not involve surface emotion.

At that point the magician usually realizes that many of the emotions channelled towards the Divine really have to do with people looking for a substitute parent: they want someone to love, protect, and uphold them. An adept steps away from that parental grasping and works instead to connect with the consciousness that we call the Divine, and to connect in a way that is not so geared towards human needs, fears, and wants.

Learning how emotions can trip up the magician, and how unbalanced emotive connections can be abused and parasited, is very important, so there are many parts of the course that work with this dynamic. It is approached in many different ways, and with slow, steady exposure. Overriding a lifetime of emotive programming is not easy, but it is necessary. The adept magician must transcend as much cultural, emotive, religious, and social programming as possible if they are to step into power, and into direct communion with powerful beings.

The second use of emotion in magic that trips up the apprentice is 'results' magic. You have a desire, and you do some magical act to fulfil it. In its basest form, results magic tends to be pretty infantile: forcing someone to love you, smiting your enemies, getting a new car, and so forth.

Results magic uses emotion as fuel for the engine , which is an exhausting and scatter-gun approach, it also quickly becomes a feeding station for hungry parasites . It is also dangerous. A person who uses rage to magically attack an enemy has already lost: the magic is often poorly thought out, and thus bounces around causing all sorts of unforeseen calamities. It also exposes the weakness within the magician: if you are ruled by your emotions, then you can be ruled. Emotions catch us off-guard, and they make us act unwisely in many ways. And a soup made of unwise acts, emotion, parasites, and unthinking spontaneity with no long-term planning is a recipe for disaster. It is all about want, not necessity; and a being, inner contact, or *another magician* can spot this weaknesses in you easily and magically manipulate you to bring you down. This does not mean that magicians should not have emotion: that would be silly, and it would deny our humanity. But the magician must learn early on that emotions often have no place in magic. Internal discipline, focus, and necessity drive powerful magic; not wants, emotions, or outbursts.

3.12   Reading and learning

Many people have asked me about whether they have to remember everything they read on the course, and how they will be tested. Many students are fearful at first that they will not retain everything. Not only is there a lot of information in the course itself, but there are also extensive reading tasks, where the student has to delve into classical and ancient writings as well as history, cultural geography, and so forth. So take notes as you go!

When a student reaches the Initiate level of their training and they wish to be mentored then their work will be tested and challenged: their notes will be looked at, and they will have some discussions with an adept. Many new students are fearful that they will not remember everything they have read, and will fail this process.

A lot of this fear comes from people who have been through the university system, or who have taken magical training where they were expected to cram for exams and written tests. Quareia does not work this way at all.

This course exposes you to a lot of different things that you have to take in, and you are introduced to some books that can be pretty dense and hard-going, particularly the Classical ones. These are not for you to revise, remember, and quote back to us; rather the intent is to expose you to something different, something that will change you at a deep level. You are often given only sections of books to read, and usually they are good books to have around for future reading. Read the indicated sections, take notes, and then, most importantly, think about what you have read in the context of magic.

The information will go in and percolate at a deep level, and when it mixes with your direct experiences then it will change you and deepen your understanding. It is your understanding that is challenged: you are not going to be tested on your texts like in college; rather a mentor speaks to you to see whether your understanding is dawning slowly, in layers.

If you are not being mentored, it is still about the change the studies create in you. Your studies are for *you*, for *your* alchemical evolution; you do not need to prove anything to anyone else. It is about the shifts and dawnings within you. Having to go through different texts yourself, rather than simply having bites of information fed to you, will teach you to spot peripheral information and knowledge. Of course you may get distracted down a side alley at times, but that too may lead you to an inspiration, which will further widen your view, internally and intellectually.

And you may get a layer of meaning that someone else will not. The Mysteries are not called Mysteries without good reason: they are woven layers of wisdom, experience, inspiration, and transformation; and they are always individual to each of us, even though together we form a collective. You will get what is necessary for you at each moment. When you return to a text a few years later, you will see other layers that you did not spot before.

3.13   The horizon

There is no end to one's magical training. There is never a pinnacle that you can reach and think, you have got there, you can stop learning because you now know everything about magic. You *never* get there. You will always be a student, you will always be learning; and the more you learn, the more you will realize how much we just cannot comprehend. A magician has stood on an important stepping stone when he or she realizes just how little we truly know.

I am constantly being asked, particularly by magicians in their earlier stages of development, how to 'get there,' as though there was some defined endpoint where someone has become an adept and has 'power.' The need for a horizon and a final destination, which is so inherent within us, has been a major influence on how magical lodges and groups have organized themselves and their paths of development.

Training groups, lodges, and organizations generally have clearly defined steps of training. Exams, hierarchies, and grades encourage a budding magician to study, strive, and achieve. The effect of such a path leads to magicians approaching magic like a college or university course. If they do the study, pass the exam, and get their certificate, then they will be a magical adept. It's an easily understood, predictable path to walk, and it gives the magician a sense of control: 'if I pay for a course and study, then I will get there.' Nothing could be further from the truth.

The reality is very different and unpredictable. Of course study is a major part of the magical path. But the study that is required is not just magical theory: you need a much wider net of knowledge that encompasses ancient history, medicine, biology, philosophy, religious texts, geometry, archaeology... the list is endless.

When someone starts along the more serious path of magical awakening, the climb up the mountain before them is steep indeed. And the mountain's summit is but a resting place for an adept before they launch into their next layer of learning. In truth, walking the Path of Hercules up the mountain is the achievement of the adept, not reaching its summit. Magic is constant death and renewal, an unpredictable force that flows like water, finding its own route, and it frequently changes its path according to land, weather, and creatures. It is a living force that cannot be contained or controlled.

> Hidden in a dark tree is a golden bough, golden in leaves and pliant stem, sacred to Persephone, the Underworld's Juno. All the groves shroud it, and shadows enclose the secret valleys. But only one who's taken a gold-leaved fruit from the tree is allowed to enter earth's hidden places.
>
> — *Virgil*, Aeneid, *Book VI.*

If a person truly wants to evolve within Magic and penetrate even a small fragment of Her Mysteries, then they must forge their magical path while they wander through the forest of life. There are no short cuts, no 'destination.' Magic is constantly all around you: the key is to pay attention.

Stillness, observation, and listening are the main skills a magician needs in their early stages. When someone wakes up to the path of magic, that awakening does not go unnoticed. Inner beings begin to draw close, to watch you, and to place things, people, and events in your path to help you take your next step forward. If you are too busy drawing out impressive sigils, scouring grimoires, or ironing your new robe that has magical script all along the hem, then you will miss the quiet voice that says 'hey, look at this: it's important' or 'go and make contact with that person: its important.'

Magical learning is a series of stepping stones that can often appear random and unconnected. And it can take you many years before you can look back on your path and see how your steps were in fact all well defined, necessary, and led you to points of major learning and/or training—and all without your realizing it at the time.

Sometimes you will come across teachers—and not all teachers are obvious—who will come into your life for a while and teach you a great deal. Some of their lessons will be useful, and some will not. There will be teachers who you will not recognize as teachers: you will meet, shake hands, make eye contact, maybe have a single conversation, and then part ways. You will not recognize for a long time that your meeting marked a major turning point and that something, some knowledge, some connection, was transferred to you in that shared moment.

Perhaps you miss a train and end up waiting in a bookshop. A book catches your eye and you buy it. It sits on your shelf, maybe for years, before you pick it up. Then you pick it up at the right time and begin to read. What you learn, or what unfolds from that book, will lay down another stepping stone. Or perhaps you have a deep instinct to read a book, which you do, and it makes no sense to you but something within you tells you that it is important.

Many years later the knowledge in that text suddenly unlocks for you, and understanding falls into place.

Occasionally the nudges from the inner beings can be insistent and if you do not get it, they will start shouting… Say an object comes your way, something strange or interesting. You have no idea about it other than you like it. It goes in a cupboard and you get on with your life. Then one day you start to see references to that type of object everywhere you turn. So you retrieve it from your cupboard and put it out, where you can see it. A few days or months later, you come across a text or teacher explaining what that object is, and how it works magically. Bingo! It was waiting patiently for you to join up the dots.

Once that door is open, the door of contact, whether you are aware of it or not, magic will begin seeping into your life. Your studies will help you and give you some foundation tools to work with, but beyond that it is about learning to listen, observe, explore, experiment, and practice. And above all, be truthful to yourself.

A noble inner shrine waits for you too in our kingdom. There, gracious one, I will place your oracles, and mystic utterances spoken to my people, and consecrate picked men. Only do not write your verses on the leaves, lest they fly, disordered playthings of the rushing winds: chant them from your mouth.

— Virgil, The Aeneid, *Book VI.*

Chapter Four

Meditation Issues

*To make no mistakes is not in the power of man; but from
their errors and mistakes the wise and good learn wisdom
for the future.*

— *Plutarch*

The biggest stumbling block for a lot of people when starting
their Quareia training is meditation, which is one of the main
cornerstones of magic. Meditation teaches you two essential and
necessary magical skills: focus and stillness. Focus is the ability to
direct your thoughts and actions with absolute precision; stillness
is the ability to stop what you are doing at any time and become
silent and still within, quickly and efficiently.

These skills do not come overnight; they come with years
of practice. Once you have gained some basic competency in
them, the course then steers you towards other simple forms of
meditation, such as meditation with your eyes open, meditation
while you walk, and short but deeply silent meditation which
lasts for a few minutes or less.

Meditation appears in Western culture in all sorts of ways, and
is used for all sorts of reasons. The techniques taught in various
schools of meditation can be complex or geared towards a specific
goal. The approach in Quareia is different: the meditation in the
course is one tool out of many, not a destination in itself. It is a
tool that enables you to *do* something.

Most events that require an adept to work within a magical
pattern come with little warning. Magic does not conveniently
confine itself to Tuesday afternoons in your temple; it is part of
your life. Sometimes danger approaches quickly and unseen. If
you regularly work with stillness then you will feel its approach.

If you regularly meditate in some form then you can fall silent within, focus quickly, and respond in an appropriate manner instead of being swept up with the approaching danger.

Being still allows you to bathe in the silence; and being in the silence within allows you to hear and feel subtle changes around you. Once you have touched truly deep silence, you will find that you can withdraw to it quickly while still functioning physically in everyday life. Getting to that point can take a long time for some, and not so long for others, but it is a natural state within you that, once touched and awakened in your conscious mind, will change you forever.

Stillness is doubly important in styles of magic which use visionary work. The mind and the imagination are the most powerful tools in magic, but for them to stay in good health, stillness needs to be part of the picture.

4.1   The stages of development

One of the big mistakes people make when they embark on meditation as part of their magical training is that they assume it is easy, as loads of people seem to be able to do it. But it is not easy; it is the hardest skill you will ever try to learn. It can quickly become a battle of wills if you are not careful. So here is a breakdown of the various stages people go through with meditation. Not everyone will go through each stage, and some people will have more difficulty with certain stages than others; but what follows should give you an idea of what can happen during your meditation, and how to develop and move forward.

And the word 'develop' should be imprinted upon your brain: a magician is a *Developing One*, and undertaking serious training means stepping off the treadmill of mundane life and stepping onto a path of constant development that does not end, not even when you die.

The movement and the noise

For a lot of people, once you sit down to be quiet and meditate, your body and mind seem to wake up. Your body wants to fidget, and your mind starts to chatter. Some people make the mistake of using music or guided meditation recordings to overcome this.

Remedies:

1. Set smaller goals if you are having too much difficulty: start at three or five minutes for each session, and build up from there.

2. Make your meditation exercise simply about shutting your eyes and sitting. Various aspect meditations are taught in the beginning of the course, which will give your mind something to think about. Training the mind is like training a feral toddler.

3. Try sitting and counting to ten (or whatever number you wish to work with). If your mind wanders by number five, then go back to number one and start again.

4. Passive meditation can help your meditation proper.

Passive meditation is where you do not sit down to meditate, but you do something that has only one focus, without any other distraction. It is a step towards meditation, and a good exercise for the mind in its own right. Passive meditation includes things like lying down and listening to a voice only (no music) meditation or self-hypnosis recording, or lying down and listening to calm music (with no voice) with eyes closed so that only your hearing sense is working. It can also be reading a book with no other distractions: no television, music, or other background noise (and your phone switched off). Learning to focus your senses on one specific thing at a time is both helpful for meditation and calming to the mind in a world that is overloaded with sensory input.

The goal

Having goals is generally good for you, but in meditation it can have the opposite effect. It can set you up for failure, for struggle, and for reaching a 'destination' which runs counter to meditation being a journey, not an arrival. Simply take each day as it comes, and be aware of distractions around you in everyday life that you had become accustomed to. Being aware of the constant noise around you (televisions, phones, stereos, etc.) helps you realize how little peace and quiet your mind and body really get every day. The rest is a new journey each day.

The lapsing and wandering mind

Once you are able to sit down and meditate a little, your conscious mind often gets bored, and will try to amuse you by digging up memories or thinking about things in general. Focus on the meditation task in hand. It can also be helpful to develop a simple mantra or keyword that you think to yourself every time you find yourself wandering. The word 'silence' is a good one, as it is a reminder and also a command. If you use it every time you wander in your mind then it will become engrammed into your consciousness, so that when you are in a loud and busy place and you need to focus, simply saying the word 'silence' to yourself will start to trigger the process of becoming still even in the midst of chaos.

The illusions

This is a problem that often comes up for beginners: as you try to be still and silent, you start to imagine 'presences' or powers around you. As a beginner, you are not capable of differentiating between real contact and your mind simply amusing itself. Also, as a beginner, it is easy to follow a distraction and not have boundaries.

When you are meditating, that is all you are doing; nothing more. So anything that presents itself to you as a 'presence' or anything else is simply distracting you. Focus on the task in hand, and do not allow your mind to follow any form of distraction, even if it seems to be deep and meaningful. This is about discipline and focus, not about giving the dramas of your mind a platform to amuse your ego.

The arrogance

This issue can creep in at the beginning of any sort of training, and can be particularly damaging if it is allowed to emerge in magical training. Arrogance in meditation is where the student finds meditation somewhat easy, tries to go longer and longer with it, and feels superior because they can meditate for hours at a time.

Long meditation sessions are used in certain Eastern sects, but they are not valuable in magic, and can end up being counterproductive. Do not to try meditating in silence for as long as possible; aim for twenty minutes to an hour. This exercise is not about withdrawing into yourself and turning away from the world; it is about being able to be still *within* the world.

High achieving or particularly driven students can be tempted to push an exercise to its, and their own, limits. Then the act of meditation becomes a challenge of endurance. The student takes pride in the fact that they have meditated for hours, and begins to feel special. They forget that the point of the exercise is to learn how to become still and silent in a split second, and how to maintain that stillness and silence in their minds as they walk down a street.

Lengthy meditation sessions have their uses, but not ones that are valuable in magic. Going too deep or for too long on a regular basis will bring about changes that are likely to be detrimental to the magician. Sprinters and marathon runners must train differently, each according to their needs. The student magician needs to develop the ability to focus at speed, to touch the stillness quickly, and to maintain that stillness while they act. The 'inner muscle' necessary for doing that is different from the 'inner muscle' developed through lengthy meditation sessions. And the student needs to treat each exercise as a stepping stone, not as an end in itself or a badge of honour to be won.

Touching the stillness

This stage of development in meditation can come at any time. For some it can come quickly, and for others it can take longer. It is irrelevant how long it takes for this experience to emerge, and you cannot force it: it will open out when the time is right in your life. Meditating simply makes it easier to move closer to that state, and gives you the skill to maintain a presence in the stillness.

The key is that your first experience of it becomes a 'marker point' where you feel total silence, timelessness, and expanse. Once you experience it, you can recover the feeling within you simply by remembering it. And this is a key to achieving silence: you are not learning it, you are remembering it.

It does not always come from meditation, it can happen in other ways too; but once experienced it can become a state of mind that can be recalled. The more it is revisited, the stronger it becomes.

Refuge

Once a student becomes comfortable with meditation and can sit quietly in stillness, it can become a bit of a refuge from the crazy world outside. While this is not a problem in itself, it is important to remember that a magician, for the most part, works out in the world, not in a withdrawn state. If you can only be still and silent in refuge, then you will have problems with your magical work.

Because of this, the course includes meditation tasks, particularly later on, where you have to meditate around noise, people, and chaos. First you learn to meditate in silence; then you learn to meditate in noise. This teaches you to be still in a crisis, so that you can touch base with the silence and stillness while still functioning in an emergency.

If you find yourself seeking refuge in meditation, don't fight that; simply balance it with meditation in a busy chaotic place, and ensure that refuge is not something that you constantly seek.

Understanding necessity

One of the later stages of development in meditation is understanding necessity that is individual to you. There are many schools of thought about meditation, and they will all give you different advice about how to meditate, how long for, and so forth. This form of blanket advice may work for people in a religious, mystical, or health setting, but what works for magicians will vary according to the individual.

By the time you reach your adept training, you will have learned through experience, and also through divination, when is best for you to meditate, how long for, and which approach (short, long, silent, noisy, etc.) to use in which circumstances, as it becomes highly variable.

Sometimes it is not a good idea to meditate, for a variety of reasons. There are times, for your safety and invisibility, when you should not be still, but be as mundane as possible. There are times when you should withdraw into meditation. And there are times where you will need to use silence while out in the world to affect everything around you.

The use of meditation as a tool becomes very individual for each magician after certain skills have been achieved: flexibility, individuality, and common sense should then be your main guides.

4.2   Questions

What about Kundalini?

I have received endless questions about whether the Apprentice Module I meditations will 'raise' Kundalini energy. The short answer is no: these meditations are there as specific tools, and anything else is a distraction. In a world saturated with the concepts of 'abundance' and instant gratification, and stuffed full of wildly overstated 'products,' people can find it hard to accept a simple exercise as just that.

The subtlety of simplicity can get lost in people's minds in such a culture, which blocks them from deriving the real benefit and skill that can be drawn from such a simple exercise. The same applies to similar questions regarding the 'third eye.'

People have been programmed to think about the glittery, exciting aspects of meditation, and that its heights can be reached almost instantly. It can be quite a struggle for some magicians to pull away from the dangerous lure that is the glamour of power. The promise of instant enlightenment or 'bliss' is a subtle promise of power, and is the very first stumbling block of the student magician.

I already do meditation but I do it differently. Do I still have to do the apprentice meditation exercises?

The short answer is yes. The meditation exercises in your early Apprentice training are there for two reasons. The first and most obvious one is to get people used to regular meditation, to learn to sit down, shut up, and focus on stillness. The second and more pertinent answer to this question is that these specific meditations pave the way for other things to come. They are kindergarten exercises that prepare for work not directly linked to meditation; forerunner exercises that prepare the mind to work with power.

I am having trouble meditating for a long time because of my work and life commitments. And yet I want to progress through the course. What can I do?

This can be a tough one for many people, as today we often live in a hamster wheel society where we work long hours and then come home to more work with our children and family. In an ideal situation, you would have thirty to forty-five minutes a day to meditate.

We do not always live in that ideal situation, so you have to adjust. There are some key things to think about when you adjust your meditation time to fit with your life. The first key thing is *avoidance*: we often subconsciously rebel against meditation because of the changes it brings. It is a regular discipline, and all discipline is something we fight against in some way or another. If you are actually just trying to fool yourself into thinking that you do not have the time for meditation, then spot that and *make* time, regardless of how much some part of you wants not to do it.

If you really cannot dedicate a good slice of time to meditation each day, then break the task up across the day. I did this when my children were little: I meditated little and often, ten minutes or more in the morning with the flame before I got the kids up, five minutes as I sat on the bus to work, and five minutes before I went to sleep. You do not always have to sit before a candle in a quiet room, so long as you do at least one session a day before the flame. I took every opportunity I could to meditate, whether it was in a waiting room, at a street corner on a bench, or in a magical space. Use your common sense, and do not fool yourself. Your aim is to be able to sit in stillness and silence for around thirty minutes. Once you can do that, then how you maintain the skill is up to you. This is *your* training: you decide upon your own success or failure.

Do I have to use a candle flame, it is distracting.

Yes, you do. Working with fire and flame is a major part of magic, and being able to be still before a flame is a basic skill that you will need.

If the flame distracts you, then get over it: you are an adult, so act like one. If you are so easily distracted, then how on earth will you cope with holding a focused contact with an inner being? As an adept you will need to be able to go into stillness and then into vision in a busy street, while walking or talking to someone. This basic meditation exercise is the very first practice of focus. Everything is in the course for a reason: you cannot cherry-pick aspects of serious training while thinking that you know better.

Do I have to meditate every day?

In the beginning, yes. Throughout your Apprentice training, having a regime of meditation that works with your life is very necessary. Things then shift in the Initiate section, and the method of meditation changes to teach you another level of focus. After the Apprentice section, how you manage your meditation routine is up to you, but it is highly recommended that you continue some form of daily meditation to keep your inner and outer balance.

When such a discipline is kept up, when you miss a few days you will really feel the difference. But to get to that stage, you have to have laid a strong foundation of meditation that in turn brings about subtle but major shifts in how you handle power. Over the years I have approached it in different ways according to what was happening in my life. Again, use your common sense, and don't fool yourself.

4.3 Summary

Keep it simple. Don't be tempted to use gadgets, herbs (or other substances), sound recordings, bells, singing bowls, or anything else. There are no shortcuts, no distractions, and no product to buy. Just sit down in a quiet space, close your eyes, and gently, slowly, teach your mind that it is okay not to be chattering all the time.

The end of the Work is unattainable.
There is no Worker complete in his Radiance.

— The Instruction of Ptahhotep

Chapter Five

Tarot

Happy the person who has learned the cause of things and has put under his or her feet all fear, inexorable fate, and the noisy strife of the hell of greed.

— *Virgil*

5.1   Issues, problems and approaches

This chapter looks at issues, problems, and approaches to do with tarot, and some questions that have been posed on the subject by various students. I have also included various extracts from my blog in this chapter for those who have not found it, and also to have all the advice in one place for students.

Of all the core skills learned in Apprentice training, tarot divination is the one that it is advisable to *play* with. The more you do it, the more you will start to understand what you are working with, and how to draw meaning from it.

The one approach to tarot not used in Quareia, and that is currently popular in tarot circles, is the use of tarot for psychological counselling. While tarot readings can touch on or expose current psychological issues, this is a side alley of divination training that it is wise not to get stuck down as a magician. Tarot for a magician is used as a pair of eyes that can see into narrow aspects of the past, present, and future; it can also be used to converse with inner contacts, to check magical patterns for integrity, and to seek out what has been hidden. These skills develop slowly over the course of the training, and cannot truly be developed if tarot is approached as a psychological tool, which is not its true purpose.

The course's tarot training starts by looking at the inner energetic aspects of your surroundings, then slowly works outwards to other subject matter and approaches. Later the magician is trained to work with a specific magician's deck: *LXXXI The Quareia Magician's Deck*. They learn to work with its cards not only for divination, but also as windows for inner contacts and anchors for power points.

5.2 Working with a deck

At the beginning of the course, in Apprentice Module I: Core skills, the student is directed to get a Rider-Waite deck to work with. This deck is only used specifically in the Apprentice section of the course, but it is an important milestone deck for magical apprentices to work with in their early training. Don't be tempted to use a different deck at this stage, as the Rider-Waite is prescribed for particular reasons.

The Rider-Waite deck, on which many other tarot decks have been based, is not the perfect deck to work with, but it is a good foundation deck, as it draws from images and concepts deeply rooted in Western magic. It also passively teaches the student about the four elemental powers and energies, and how those elemental powers of Air, Fire, Water, and Earth are expressed in magic.

The symbolism in the Rider-Waite deck is also something that needs to be learned passively by using the deck. It is the language of the outer court of the Western Mysteries, and while the understanding of that symbolism has largely fallen by the wayside and been replaced by psychological interpretations, the deck's images still speak for themselves.

The cards themselves are not deep mystical powers; they are simply a vocabulary, an alphabet that the brain can use to decipher what your consciousness is reaching for. When you do a reading to look into the future, you are tapping into a pattern of energy. Without a vocabulary to decipher what you are looking at, the patterns are meaningless.

I can remember, at the tender age of fourteen or fifteen, laying out the major cards of the Rider-Waite in their numerical order. I 'knew' there were deeper meanings behind the images and the order in which they came; I 'knew' that if I could just penetrate that hidden variable then I would become 'wise.' It took me many years before I could lay out the cards in the same way and think, 'yeah, some interesting patterns, but the designers were limited in their thinking as far as magical development goes.' Now my opinion is, 'yeah, a bit useful, but…whatever.' It is an early developmental tool in magic—not the most powerful or profound thing you will ever work with, but a key component of the early stages of your training, nevertheless.

What a Rider-Waite tarot deck does is give shapes to the energies in the orbit of the Western Mysteries, so that you can translate them into meanings that you can grasp. Just as a farmer watches the behaviour of the birds, trees, and creatures to decide what weather is coming over the next couple of months, so the tarot reader lays out cards in a defined way to discern what patterns are currently in play and what their longer-term effect will be. More importantly, tarot also indicates what deeper powers are at play, using the visual vocabulary of the Western Mysteries. It is not the best magical vocabulary, which is why you only use it as an apprentice, but it is a foundational starting point for understanding.

The best way to learn that vocabulary is to get to know the cards. Lay them out, group the families together, look at their images and numbers, get to know their personalities. Look through whatever book comes with the deck and look at the pictures. Choose a key word or two for each card based on the information you have, and write that keyword on the card (or on a bit of tape stuck to it).

Just as a child learns to read by recognizing single words at a time and may not get the whole sentence in one go, so a new tarot reader needs to learn their key words for each card. Don't dive into the mystical magical aspects of the card; just get to know its surface presentation to start with.

Do simple readings, lots of them, until you are familiar with the deck and with some layouts, and write down your results. Later, go back and reread your notes. Look at the readings you did, then compare them with what actually happened. This is how you truly begin to learn your vocabulary, as well as the deck.

5.3 Uses of tarot

Most people think of tarot as useful only for looking into the future and for psychological counselling. These are only two uses of this tool; there are many. Tarot can also be used to look at a present situation or a past situation, and as a shared vocabulary to speak to inner beings, spirits, and deities.

Why would you want to look at the here and now if you are already in it? Oh, many reasons. You could check on a missing child, look at the inner powers and hidden agendas behind a current situation, or investigate the suitability of a candidate. Tarot can used to throw light on a past event or person to help us better understand a past situation that is still unfolding in the present. Really there is no limit to what can be looked at; however, the accuracy and detail you can obtain from a reading depends on your ability to interpret objectively: you have to detach yourself from the situation.

5.4 The skill of interpretation

For people trying to learn tarot, the key is not just learning the deck's meanings, but also how to interpret readings. It is a skill that takes time and practice to develop, and for some it is easier than others. If you are used to viewing the world or taking in information in a 'black-or-white' way, then learning tarot will likely be a difficult task.

Interpretation uses the same mental skill as observing patterns. Just as a child learns to read the nuances of a human face and the emotions it expresses, so a reader has to learn the subtleties of each card and the patterns that they work within. It is not a skill that can be book-studied then applied in all its glory: like all aspects of magic, tarot truly is an art form that takes practice to develop properly.

All interpretation needs boundaries if it is not to devolve into flights of fancy. The boundaries that tarot operates within are context, specific questions, and time spans.

Let's have a look at a practical example. A person, let's call him Bill, buys a tarot deck, settles himself down, and decides to have a look at his future. So Bill shuffles like fury and asks the question, 'what does the future hold for me?.' He lays out the cards, and the last card—the answer card—is Death. Immediately panic sets in, and Bill freaks out.

So what went wrong here? Well, nothing, really. Bill asked what the future holds for him, and death is the inevitable outcome for us all. His question was too far-reaching, too vague. Once he has calmed down, Bill decides to try another question. 'What job should I do?' Bill lays out the cards, but he is totally unable to make any sense out of the various cards that present themselves. He is still no wiser as to what the future holds for him or what direction should he go.

The cards do not have a sufficiently specific vocabulary to answer that sort of question: there is no card for 'you should be a welder,' or 'you should be an analyst.' You have to learn to pose questions that the cards can answer.

If Bill had asked something like 'Show me what major events will happen in my life over the next five years,' then he would have been shown the events in that timeframe that would have had the most impact on him. If he had asked the same question with a timeframe of twelve months, then he would have been shown the major and not-so-major events of that twelve-month period. The narrower the timeline for a reading, the more everyday, mundane situations will show. In a three-month reading, the Tower card can be anything from a serious catastrophe to merely *feeling* that the world is crashing down on you when it's not. A bad headache, bumping your car, or an upsetting argument—all these can show as the Tower in small time frames. With longer timeframes it is more likely saying, 'the destruction of something is ahead.' This could be the loss of a job, the break up of a relationship, or a storm that takes your roof off.

Having said this, an anomaly that can show in time defined readings is the showing of something big which is beyond the timeframe. When you limit the reading to a particular timeframe and nothing really is happening within it, but something much bigger, perhaps something life-changing, lies ahead beyond the timeframe, then it can sometimes show up.

The keys to narrowing things down and obtaining more specific answers are your choices of question and layout. When you see something major in a long-term reading, you can then use a layout of one card for each time unit—a month, a year—to narrow down when a particular event is likely to hit. So for example if you see something that looks pretty bad, and you need to know when it is likely to hit, then laying out a line of cards—twelve cards for the next twelve months, ten cards for the next ten years—will likely show you when the problem will occur. When you use a timeline of cards, make sure you are specific about when the timeline starts. For example, if you have seen a major incident in a long-term reading and you want to narrow down when it is likely to strike, and you wish to check the next ten years, then shuffle the cards while asking, 'which year will this event likely happen,' and also define in your mind that the first card you lay down is your current year, and each subsequent card is for each year that follows.

The further away in time a situation shows, the more likely it is that you can take evasive action now. Fate is like a series of intersecting roads: the further away something is, the more likely there are to be other paths that you can take. When something shows in a reading in the more distant future, the seeds of that event are already in your sphere—you are walking a path towards it already. By changing something in your present—plans, courses of action, behaviour—you can shift the path of your future.

This is a particularly important skill for magicians, as it also teaches you not to panic when you see bad things on the horizon. Put it in context. When you go to cross the road and you see a truck coming down the road quickly, you do not panic; you simply change your intention to cross the road at that point and you wait until it has passed. Life is full of good, bad, and mixed events, and they all have purposes to some extent. The difference between a magician and a mundane person is that the magician can see some things coming, and they can wait for them to pass, get out of the way, or change course. Some bad events cannot be avoided: those are often ones that you can draw a lot of learning from. Still, forewarned is forearmed, and you can make sure you are in a good position to weather the storm and draw as much learning as possible from it.

Treat tarot, and divination in general, like everything else in life: it can be terrifying and daunting at first, but once you begin to grasp the skill you start to learn from your experiences, and you learn that not all bad things are really bad. Treat learning divination as being like a child learning to play out on their own for the first time. It can be stressful and everything can be perceived as a threat to start with. But as you learn to interpret, you become more comfortable with the readings, and you can look, decipher, and act as though they were everyday things.

Choosing the right layout and the right question is always the key. A layout that is too detailed is often not helpful unless you need an absolute overview—which for a lot of things, you do not. If your layout is not detailed or specific enough, then you will only get vague information or an overview.

Shuffling is also important. People forget that how you shuffle is a major part of your success at reading cards. Some people will halfheartedly jumble the cards around as they chat or watch television! If you are not focused then your reading will not be properly focused. Close your eyes to shut out the world, think only of the question as you shuffle, and learn to feel the cards 'finding' their own places. When every card is where it needs to be, you will not shuffle any more: you will feel that they are done. They do not need 'cutting': you are not playing poker. Once they are all in place, simply put them down and start laying them out.

But what layout to use? Every layout has its strengths and weaknesses. And the layout needs to be relevant to the question: many experienced readers will have quite a few different layouts that they use to get specific answers. I use health layouts, layouts for magical questions, a specific layout for yes/no answers, a layout for energetic details, and a specific layout for when I need a lot of information.

Let's go back and revisit Bill, who is still struggling with his readings. He is at a job crossroads and wants to know what he should be doing in the future. Rather than asking the open-ended question that he originally attempted, Bill has now decided to think a bit more carefully. He has several career options open to him, so he writes them down as questions:

1. *Should I stay with the company I am currently working for?*

2. *Should I go back to college and study nursing, which I have always wanted to do?*

3. *Should I take the job offer to work in the local store that I was offered?*

4. *Should I go self-employed?*

These are four distinct questions, but he still has not really focused them properly. He has asked 'should I?' but what does 'should' really mean here? Is he concerned with his finances? Is he concerned with his satisfaction and happiness? First, Bill needs to think about what he wants from a job, and why is he looking for change. Bill decides that he is looking for satisfaction and happiness: he has a well-paid job at the moment, but he is deeply unhappy. He is willing to take a pay cut to be happy, if that is what it takes.

Bill decides to use the Tree of Life layout. With this layout, the last card is the answer, and the other cards are the details of how that answer happens. So he asks his first question. The last card is the Tower. It is a simple answer: no matter what other cards appear, the outcome is shit, so it is best not even to consider that option.

He asks question two, still using the Tree of Life layout. Here the answer is a bit broader. The cards that fall in their specific positions tell him that he will mentally enjoy the challenge (Three of Pentacles in the eighth position), that he will make friends and enjoy the experience (Four of Wands in the seventh position), and that he will struggle financially (Five of Pentacles in the ninth position); but for the outcome, he would be disappointed and most likely will have a bad time in his eventual job or may not even get one at all (Ten of Swords in the tenth position).

Bill asks about option three, the local store job, and again uses the same layout. In the ninth position is the Magician, and in the tenth position is the Ace of Cups. The fourth position, the new path forging ahead, has Five of Pentacles. The fifth position, 'withheld,' has the Ten of Swords, and the seventh position has the Three of Cups. In his store job, Bill would have a limited income—Five of Pentacles—but he would love the job and the hours—Three of Cups. He would learn a lot he didn't expect to learn—Magician in the ninth position—and he would be nourished by the job—Ace of Cups. The Tree of Life layout, which you learn in the course, gives straightforward answers. When you need more detail and more specifics, the Landscape layout (also in the course) gives you more information about specific aspects of the situation. When the question is mundane, the positions of the layout have simple meanings. When the question is magical, there are layers to each position. The skill of interpreting these layers comes from practice and experience.

5.5   Interpreting the cards

At first the vast array of meanings for each card can be confusing and overwhelming. To get basically proficient, it is best to narrow each card down to a key word or phrase, then look at the pictures. Using the Rider-Waite deck is good for this, as the card pictures are simple and straightforward. Someone has a bundle of sticks on their back—Nine of Wands—so they have a burden. What that burden *is* depends on the question and where it lands in a layout. If you are asking about a job and that card turns up in a relationship position, then it could mean that your relationship will have problems if you take that job, or that you will have burdens of difficulty with someone in the job itself. To narrow that down, you would then do a yes/no reading to ask how that job would affect your relationship with your partner. If it shows no particular problem, then you know the issue would be with someone at work. It is all about context, common sense, and simplicity.

For example, in a reading, the King of Pentacles can mean a man of wealth, finances, or property; or it can mean an ancestor or male elder within your family or community. If your question is about work or money, then it probably indicates a boss or financial advisor who is experienced. If you are asking a magical question then it could indicate an ancestor or older man an astrological earth sign. The real key is to make sure that your interpretation is relevant to the question. Don't interpret a card magically when you are asking about something mundane.

The more you work with simple word keys for each card, the more confident you will become. Your natural ability will slowly take over, and over time you will find that your own meanings develop for each card. With practice and time, you will become far more proficient at the subtleties of interpretation. You will also develop natural inner sight, which will further expand your ability to interpret the cards.

Remember when you first learned to drive and you were like an accident waiting to happen? But over time you developed your own driving style, and now you can drive without having to think about every action, every person on the road, every junction, sign, or other car. You work on autopilot and process lots of input at high speed: the same goes with tarot. Do lots of readings, write them down—then return to them after some time has passed. One of the greatest habits for effective learning is to make good use of hindsight. In the case of tarot, revisiting your old readings will often shed new light on what the cards were trying to tell you.

Tarot is a language, a vocabulary, and like all languages it has to be learned properly, then used frequently to build your fluency and sensitivity to its nuances. The attitude of 'oh, I don't need to bother learning it properly because I can just look up the meaning of each card,' makes about as much sense as expecting to be able to have deep and meaningful conversations in a language you do not speak because you have bought yourself a dictionary.

5.6 Looking at the present and the issue of privacy

When my kids were teens they were pretty good, and they would let me know if they were going to be home late so that I would not worry. One evening my daughter went to the local festival. She had agreed to be in by 10 p.m.. It got to 10:30 p.m. and there was still no sign of her. This was before the days when every living creature had a cellphone. I began to panic. By 11 p.m. I was ready to call the police, as it was so unusual for her to be so late. But before I did that, I did a reading to see if she was okay. I used the Tree of Life and asked 'what is she doing at this moment in time.' Posing the question clearly is of the utmost importance.

The last card was the Chariot: she was in a car travelling somewhere. So I did a second reading and asked if she was in danger. The last card was the World: no, she was not in danger, she was busy enjoying the world. She finally came through the door twenty minutes later and was very apologetic. She had lost track of time as she was enjoying herself so much. I wanted to be angry with her, not because she had committed some terrible crime but because I had been out of my mind with worry. But we had a simple chat, and we worked out a strategy to avoid such a situation happening again. As a teen, she could not understand my panic, but she respected it. As an adult, I had to remember those heady moments of teenage joy when one forgets the mundane. I knew from her reading that she was being honest with me; and I, as a card-reading mother, had to be strict with myself about respecting her privacy.

Respecting people's privacy is important with tarot, especially with readings about the present. Be aware that it could very easily tip into spying or invading privacy and it should not be used to look at an individual without really good cause. When you develop in divination, you slowly start to realize what you can potentially do with it, and ethics of a true magical path must come into play. When it comes to your own family, then use your common sense: if it is a potential emergency, then use it. When it is not, do not spy on your family. And the same goes for readings about other people: divination can have all sorts of consequences both energetically, and in life dynamics, so tread ethically and sensibly.

When you need to practise you can use public figures: they, by nature of their job, have chosen to put their life out in the public eye. You can do readings about them, and in hindsight you will discover whether you were right about what the cards were telling you.

Many years ago I was teaching a tarot workshop in the USA at election time, and we looked at Bill Clinton. It showed him winning the election but not completing his term of office. The reading also seemed to show a hidden daughter coming to light and causing a scandal. Of course, in retrospect it turned out not to be a daughter, but a much younger woman and his hidden affair with her. This taught me that the pattern I had been interpreting as 'daughter' could simply mean a much younger woman where there was an emotional bond.

As you advance through with your training in Quareia, you will learn about weaving, connecting, and conversing with various energies. The deeper into the training you go, the more powerful your connections will become, and this will affect your divination. Your readings will become much more powerful, to the extent that sometimes you may unintentionally set up an energetic link with the situation or person you are reading about. The more empathic you are, the more easily this can happen without your realizing.

When you read for a situation, a connection can be set up. Then, every time something major happens with that situation or person, it can tug on your energies. For years I would suddenly, and for no apparent reason, lose my vital force and collapse like a house of cards. Eventually I discovered that each of those times something important had happened to someone for whom I had read: my energy had been going into them to support them at a critical time. So choose carefully what you connect with, and how much you are willing to help.

Readings for the present can also be used to look at buildings (is someone in a building that should be empty?) or to locate something. When you need to locate something specific, like a child, pet, or object, then you have to define the cards you wish to work with in your interpretation. Let me give you an example.

You lose a pet and they are in danger: you need to find them quickly. Your first reading would ask, 'what direction should I look in to find X.' You would use a four-directional layout, and the first or last card for the centre (you define which), so five cards in total. You would ask that the card indicating the right direction be a 'success' type of card.

You must set in your mind what type of card you are looking for. If you do not do this, your answer may show a disaster card if the animal is in distress, or a 'doing' card if the animal is doing something. Can you see how much you are leaving to the tarot's interpretation, if you do not define *how* you wish the correct direction to be indicated? I would look for cards that denote success, like the Sun or Six of Wands (victory). The indicated direction then becomes the starting point: the next reading would ask, 'if I go and look in that direction, will I find them?' If the answer is no, then you need to look at whether they are trapped in a building (yes or no), are they injured, etc.

When one of my cats first came to live with me, he was a kitten, was partially blind, and had never been outdoors. Once he was introduced to the outside world through a cat flap, he went exploring. One day he vanished for several hours and I became worried. I did a directional reading which told me to look south of my house on a road with various cottages, fields, and farms. I asked whether if I looked there, I would find him. The answer was yes (Two of Pentacles, balance). I asked if he was injured. The answer was no, but that he was trapped (Eight of Swords, taken literally as a picture). So off I went, calling him loudly, checking and calling outside every garage and shed. After about twenty minutes I was a quarter of a mile south of my house, out by a farm and surrounded by fields. I heard a pitiful cry. As I got closer, I found my cat stuck fast in a hedge. It was literally the Eight of Swords: he was surrounded and trapped by thorns. I hauled him out of the brambles, and he did not wander off again for a long time.

Another time it was a family member's cat that had vanished. A series of yes/no and directional readings showed that the cat was distressed, lost, and trapped somewhere. Having used a map to located the area where I thought the cat was, I asked what sort of building the cat was in. The answer was the Hierophant, which I read to be a church. I asked if the cat would eventually make it home, and the answer came back that it would take quite a while, but he would eventually return. (I used the Landscape layout: the immediate answer was Four of Pentacles, hunkering down and holding on, while the longer-term future card was the Sun: success). So I told the person that all they could do was wait and hope for the best. Nearly three weeks later, a rather thinner, sheepish, but relieved cat wandered home.

If you use these techniques to look for a missing child, then you must detach yourself from the emotions surrounding their disappearance, otherwise you will not get a clear reading. And if you are asked to do a reading for a missing child then you have to be willing and able to share any distressing answers: you must never, ever give false hope or try and make a person feel better. It is not your place to do that. I have worked on a couple of missing children cases in the past, and I found both of them distressing. Both times it was obvious in the readings that the children were already dead, and it was more a matter of recovering remains. Sometimes the truth is not pretty, and if you want to look through the veils, you have to be mature enough to accept what you see.

5.7   Energetic hygiene

Working with tarot can sometimes get messy in terms of energetic dirt: you are dipping into reflections of fate patterns, and at times parasited situations. All this collects on your hands and on your deck. If you are not careful, the energetic dirt can build up and start to affect your physical energy, leaving you vulnerable to parasites. Simple basic magical hygiene will avoid this.

If you work a lot with one deck, then it will get too grubby to use in the long term *even if* you periodically cleanse it. Decks are tools, and at times they will need replacing, so be aware that you will eventually need to buy a replacement deck. You will feel it when the deck has become too clogged to use: it will feel grubby and your hands will feel grubby after using it.

To avoid a build-up of energetic dirt, periodically place the cards in a large dish and pour a lot of dry, finely ground, ordinary salt over the cards so that they are covered. Leave them in the salt overnight, or for at least a few hours. Then take them out and give them a good shake.

Having a cloth that is only used to keep your cards in, and to read them on, is also a good idea. It does not need to be anything special: I have used a tea towel before. You want a washable cloth to keep the cards wrapped in. When you do readings, spread it out and do the layout on it. Wash it monthly with soap and salt to keep it clean. I pop a few drops of frankincense oil on my cloth every so often, just to stop any build-up in the cloth. Don't let anyone touch or play with your cards: keep them only for your hands.

When you have finished your divination session, wash your hands immediately. Use dry salt and liquid soap to give your hands a good scrub. It is really important to make sure that any energetic residue does not stay in your hands.

In terms of keeping the 'inner air' clear while you are reading, light a candle and burn frankincense resin if you can. If you feel a bit of passive resistance in the space around you then play sacred music while you read. One of the best things I have found to play when I need clear readings is a CD recording of church bells. It has no music or other accompaniment: it's just bells, bells, bells. Sacred music will discourage any low-level parasite or local being from drawing closer and trying to interfere with your reading. This does not tend to happen a lot for apprentice-level magicians, but it can be an issue for more advanced practitioners. Beings can interfere with a reading to give you a false narrative if it is in their interests; or they may just wish to play around with you for their own amusement. Sound, smells, and a flame can discourage them.

In terms of energetic hygiene, I would caution against getting involved with public readings or 'tarot fairs' where a lot of people are doing a lot of readings: such events can quickly turn into parasite heaven. You generally leave them feeling exhausted, battered, and with a bad headache—a reaction to the inner grime that comes from a lot of mundane readings happening in a small space. Such events are not good for your long-term health, and they have no magical value at all.

A lot of tarot issues can be solved through common sense and recognizing your weaknesses. Don't be tempted to continually read for the same thing. And don't use tarot as an income source: it can make you feel grubby, tired, and depressed. This is because such a practice is not only unnecessary, but it also often draws parasites and gets you linked to all sorts of things. Remember, tarot is a magical tool: treat it with respect and use it when it is necessary, or for your learning.

5.8   Some student questions

Do I have to use the Rider-Waite deck, as I don't like it?

Yes, you do. If you don't like it, suck it up, it is part of the training. Before you can move on to using other decks (particularly *The Quareia Magician's Deck*) you need to learn the common language of tarot, which is the Rider-Waite.

You do not need to study tarot in depth or dive into the ever-growing mountain of personal psychology tarot books. But you do need to be familiar with its images and their basic meanings, as they crop up in the weirdest places. The Rider-Waite is also not an easy deck to read with, which is *good*: it forces your inner senses to work a bit harder.

Do I still have to do the tarot lessons, as I am already a tarot reader?

Sort of. A tarot reader will have the skill of divination, but they may not be familiar with the layouts and methods that are particular to Quareia and the study of magic. If you are a tarot reader then read through the lessons, do the layout exercises so that you get familiar with them, and do any of the practical work that is unfamiliar or something you do not have a strong grasp of. The patterns that appear in the tarot lessons emerge later in the course as magical power patterns, so you will need to know them and be able to work with them. View this part of the course as adding to your skills as a reader rather than replacing them.

Can I just use my own layouts/spreads for the exercises?

No. You must work with the course's spreads, as they form a foundation for later magical work. By learning the layouts, you are also learning magical patterns. Of course you may use other spreads *as well*, but you must learn the pattern language of the specific layouts in the course, as they are far more than just layouts.

Can I make my own tarot deck?

If you wish. But you must make sure that the imagery on the cards is the same: there are certain keys in the Rider-Waite that will teach you a set magical vocabulary. And to be honest, by the time you have bought the blank card stock, pens, and paints, and have spent a month painting the images, you might as well have just bought a Rider-Waite deck. It is an inexpensive deck, as it is the most common deck still in use today (and really most tarot decks used today are variants of the Rider-Waite deck).

Can I skip the tarot sections, as I don't like divination?

You cannot skip any part of the course if you want to learn magic properly. Divination is a key skill, and its applications will develop and become more complex as you progress. The course itself is ungoverned, so what you do with it is your business; but if you truly want to develop into an adept—and particularly if you want any official recognition of your achievements by Quareia—then you will need to do every part of it. The tarot lessons in the course are not there for to look pretty or to pad the course out; they are a key element of your magical training. It is also character-building to do things that you do not particularly like. When you go to university you cannot opt out of parts of your course: it would leave gaping holes in your education.

Is using a card a day a good idea?

This has become a fashion in tarot circles over the last few decades: my question is, why would you do that? If you are using tarot to find out what your day will be like, then you will miss a great many major points about learning to walk the path of the magician. It is not harmful, it can be fun and interesting, and some people do use this technique to get a heads-up for their day. But it can also become a crutch and a distraction, and something that really serves no purpose of any depth.

> The lord whose is the oracle at Delphoi neither utters nor hides his meaning, but shows it by a sign. The Sibyl, with raving lips uttering things mirthless, unbedizened, and unperfumed, reaches over a thousand years with her voice, thanks to the god in her.
>
> — *Heraclitus*

Chapter Six

Visionary Work

6.1 Issues, techniques, and questions

Glance at the sun. See the moon and stars. Gaze at the beauty of the green earth. Now think.

— *Hildegard of Bingen*

In the early stages of your training, in Apprentice Module I, you are given techniques that will prepare your mind for visionary work. In your early exercises, you are prompted to 'look in vision' around your home, your street, and so forth. This serves two main purposes: one is to prepare you for magical visionary work, and the other is to make sure that your mind works in the right way for vision work.

When we 'go into our heads,' the first layer of images, ideas, and sensations tend to come from our conscious and then our subconscious minds. A danger in the early stages of visionary training is to allow your subconscious mind to emerge and begin talking to you through imagery. While this may be useful in a psychological sense, to dig out what lurks in the dark corners of your mind, it is counterproductive in magical work.

If your subconscious is allowed or encouraged to 'play out' too much then it can become a loud voice that can be difficult get past. This can prevent the magician from casting their mind outwards into different realms.

To circumvent this problem, apprentice magicians learn the basics of using their mind for vision by casting outwards right from day one. Instead of turning inwards and allowing what wants to come up to the surface, you have to cast outwards and look at your familiar surroundings using your mind rather than your eyes. This can be difficult for some people in the early stages of their training, but it is worth the effort.

The more a student learns to cast their mind outwards, the more their 'inner muscle' grows which lets them operate first in their own familiar realm, and later, in realms beyond the physical world. By focusing their mind on imagery from their surroundings, and learning how to explore the physical world with their mind instead of their eyes, their subconscious slowly learns to stay in its place and do its job.

At first, the student will get a mix of what they have constructed from memory of their surroundings, along with bits from their subconscious, as it tries to assert imagery. But the more the mind casts outwards, the less the subconscious has a hold upon the imagery, which enables the student's deeper senses to pick up on beings, energies and constructs that have no physical form, but have a strong energetic presence.

As you progress, your inner vision will slowly start to develop until you have an experience which is clearly not being generated by your mind. This takes a lot of time, work, and effort, but it is a core skill in magic.

Some people do not see images with vision work, particularly early in their training; instead they get impressions, feelings, hunches, and so on. Some people never see any images at all, yet can function perfectly well as visionary adepts: those who do not have the faculty of seeing images in vision will find that other senses of theirs take over. As you develop in training, you will come to understand how your mind communicates information to you.

When a visionary contact is especially powerful, even the most image-strong visionary magicians may find that all imagery vanishes, to be replaced by a 'knowing.' They 'know' a being is there, what it is about, and what it is doing, but without any visual cues. This happens to me sometimes when imagery would get in the way of the contact: instead of receiving images, some deep and nameless inner sense provides all the information that is necessary for that particular working.

6.2 What is visionary magic?

Visionary magic is the use of the imagination as an interface and doorway between the physical world and the inner worlds. Our imagination makes use of 'templates' or constructs through which our consciousness can step: those templates are visions which have been worked with and built up over many generations. This is *not* psychological pathworking, though it uses similar techniques. With the psychological use of the imagination you explore yourself, and your subconscious talks to you. With visionary magic, you are exploring the non-physical worlds of which you are part.

So how does visionary magic work? Every outer manifestation of substance and power has an inner version, a version with energy and power but no physical form. Manifestation and inner pattern are always entwined, either by nature or by human design, and one drives the other. A temple, for instance, is built first in the imagination of its priests, who work to a series of magical parameters. Then the outer temple is built. One upholds the other, and allows power to flow from the inner worlds to the outer worlds. When the outer temple finally decays and falls apart, the inner pattern remains for a time before that too, begins to decay.

Working in vision, within prescribed magical patterns (templates) we can access the Inner Temples. These are structures and landscapes created by humans over long periods of time, often over many generations. We can also access the inner patterns of nature, of the land, and of consciousness. Just as the magician creates an 'inner structure' by using their mind, so Divinity creates an inner structure first, before the outer structure/life comes into being. We humans follow the same pathway of action that Divine creation uses.

The key is focus and working within the set boundaries, patterns, and structures that a particular magical or spiritual path lays down. Set keys that have been used for millennia become well-trodden paths that are safe and manageable to work with. If, on the other hand, you just play in your imagination until you manage to project yourself outwards, then you leave yourself exposed to all manner of unpleasant situations.

6.3   How do you know when it is real?

This is the age-old question asked of teachers. You will know when you have crossed over from your imagination when things start to happen that you were not expecting, and you are shown things or exposed to situations that you do not understand, or you see unusual things that other magicians are also seeing. You will see something or be told something that does not make sense, or that you do not already know about. Afterwards, sometimes quickly, sometimes months or even years later, you will then come across that 'something' in the manifest world. Perhaps you hear it described in some archaeological or scientific discovery; perhaps you come across some obscure text that describes what you saw. Or your inner contacts may make specific predictions that come true. Conformation of the inner worlds' reality can come in various ways, but however it comes, it comes when the time is right for you.

The key is to treat everything in the early stages of your work as if it were real. If you keep second-guessing and testing then you will fail, as your consciousness will be trying to control the situation. It will be clear when you eventually cross into the inner worlds: there is a massive difference between your imagination and true experience.

Magic is an art form, and like all art forms its treasures unfold slowly with time, work, and experience. You cannot speed up the process or cut corners. It is a craft that takes a long time to master. The Mysteries unfold themselves in their own time; they cannot be bought or dabbled with. That is why they are Mysteries.

6.4   The first step of visionary work

Visionary work can quickly be taken up by the mind as a browsing pastime, which must be avoided at all costs. This discipline has become much harder for young people who have been exposed to years of computer games: their minds expect to be playing and constantly changing focus. Meditation will train the mind away from these tendencies, and allow one's natural visionary skills to surface.

Before you begin to delve into magical structures, it is important to be aware of your inner surroundings: the inner manifestations of the land on which you live. The inner landscape of the land and the immediate realms surrounding that landscape are important foundations upon which any magical work must stand. It is pointless to reach for the moon before you know your own backyard. This is reflected in the early stages of training.

You must also be aware of the necessity for inner and outer boundaries. These boundaries do not have to be in place forever: indeed, the need for boundaries changes from generation to generation depending on each individual magician's consciousness and their collective culture. The course's early boundaries are there to safeguard your mind and spirit: natural visionary students can find themselves drawn to practising their visionary skills haphazardly to satisfy their curiosity or to push boundaries early on. This makes them vulnerable to parasites, feral beings, and latent imbalances within their personalities which can trigger mental illness. With visionary work comes great power, and as with wielding any great power one's mantras should be 'caution,' 'common sense,' and 'discipline.'

Once the boundaries are in place then you can begin to learn the inner highway code of conduct, the basics of 'stranger danger,' and how to tread the paths to various realms safely—or at least without too many mishaps. In times past, magical lodges put strict boundaries on where its members were permitted to travel in vision. In many of those lodges those boundaries are still in place today, but their original purpose seems to have been forgotten—as has the understanding of what magical visionary work is, and how it is done effectively.

Some lodges still use a slow and cumbersome ladder of inner contacts, as well as strict grades and top-heavy rituals. They also have an abundance of rules, regulations, and secrecy oaths. New contacts are rarely sought, and the health or balance of the current contacts is rarely challenged.

Instead, only the *information* given by the contacts is challenged— and this is usually conducted through trance mediumship with the occasional foray into vision. This way of working traps the flow of power in a small pot. The rigid reliance on a small group of recent human inner contacts, who can only be communed with inside of a tight hierarchy, eliminates the potential for deeper, older, and more profound contacts.

Some magical groups approach the visionary work as purely psychological constructs used to 'better' the student, and while that can have its uses, it is not magical visionary work, but something very different. This approach became a fashion with the rise in psychology in the early twentieth century, and although the experimentation of imaginary constructs within psychology has many uses, its cross over into magic effectively strangled both the use and understanding of magical vision

Once you have worked for any length of time with magical visionary work, you will spot countless references to it when you read classical Greek philosophers, Ancient Egyptian texts, and early Christian writings, as well as the writings of thirteenth-century Sufi mystics like Ibn Al Arabi and eighteenth-century Jewish mystics like Israel ben Eliezer (Baal Shem Tov). Once you know the work and have practical experience of it, you will start to recognize when it is being spoken about. Magical visionary work is where magic and mysticism intersect; and throughout the course you will be introduced to various Classical, ancient, and medieval writers so that you can explore their work.

With that in mind, it is really important to understand from the start that visionary work is not psychological, and should not be used for psychological purposes. Later, when you have solid visionary skills as an adept, you will be able to use your mind and imagination in all sorts of different ways, including for psychological purposes. But first you must learn the skills properly, in context, and within the boundaries of your training.

6.5   What are boundaries?

In visionary magic, the 'boundaries' are the paradigm you work in. The landscape, the images, descriptions of places and how to get to them, the descriptions of the contacts, the method for opening the contact, the method for closing the contact—all these create a working magical format to operate within. This is called 'pattern making.' The boundaries are the maps, and the maps are visionary interfaces that have been passed down by magicians, mystics, and priests for millennia.

In Quareia training, you are eased slowly into vision work, first through exploring your surroundings, then through visions that connect you to inner contacts and structures that have been used for a very long time in magical and mystical history. Safely within these boundaries you can develop your unique visionary skills, strengthen your inner abilities, and learn to interact properly with different types of beings.

When a student has a strong imagination and their conscious and subconscious mind has a vast vocabulary derived from films and games, problems can occur. I have talked about this before in this guide, and I cannot stress how important it is to recognize when this internal vocabulary makes itself known. It is bound to happen to many people, particularly early in their training, and the best way to handle it is to see the influence affecting your imagination, be aware of it, and take note. Don't fight it, but do not feed it: simply recognize what is happening and move it to one side by ignoring it. How and where you put your focus in vision trains your mind what to treat as 'contamination' and to slowly filter it out. Also, do not be distracted by things happening or appearing in the periphery of your vision in the early and middle stages of your training. Don't allow your mind to overdress something, or fill in gaps with unnecessary detail.

6.6 I cannot see anything

When an apprentice student sees nothing, they can feel like a failure and be tempted to give up. There are a couple of reasons why this problem can happen. It could be that the person has what is termed 'aphantasia': they do not have a mind's eye, and therefore cannot imagine images. Or it could be that they do have a mind's eye, but it has not been used much.

One way of determining whether your issue is aphantasia is to close your eyes and imagine a tree. Can you construct a tree in your imagination and see some basic features like its trunk and leaves? Or does your mind create a feeling or 'knowing' of a tree? If you cannot create any mental image at all, but your mind is instead providing clues, feelings, or 'knowings' that you are thinking about a tree, then you likely have some sort of aphantasia. Of course, most of us fall somewhere on the spectrum between total aphantasia and a totally photorealistic imagination.

If you find that you may be aphantasic, then you need to learn how your mind works. Close your eyes and think about a person, place, or thing that you really care about, that you know well. What tells your mind that you are thinking about that subject? Are you drawing on what you already know about them? Does it come to you in a form of just 'knowing,' or are you using a list of attributes in your head? Spend time with this, and think about how you are recovering your memories and feelings of that subject.

Then take it a step further. Think about a place you know little about and have never visited. Close your eyes and think about that place. What sort of filters for information does your mind provide? How do you 'imagine' that place? Do you get a feeling or a sense of a place; or do you form an image of a city or place? Whatever way your brain uses to reference what you are trying to imagine is the filter through which your visionary work will flow.

So for example, if you are instructed in a lesson to go in vision to the Inner Library, then some people will see in their mind's eye a building with many books in it. Others will smell the books but not see anything, and though they will be aware that 'people' are in the Library, they could not tell you what they look like. And some people will get a narrative or list in their heads: 'a place of many books, there are people there, one of them wishes to talk to me, but I don't know what they look like.'

Most people have an element of that experience. I do. I see some things very strongly, and other times I get a feeling or knowing or I get a list. But for an aphantasic, there are no visuals at all. Learn to work with what you have: aphantasics can work just as well in vision as people with strong visual skills; they simply operate in a different way.

When it is not an issue of aphantasia, it is usually a matter of an imagination that has not been used much. This is a fairly modern phenomenon, and has emerged as a result of the exteriorization of the imagination onto screens. With the advent of television, film, and computer games, a lot of imagination has become passive: you can see the characters on the screen, so you do not have imagine what they look like. This is quite an important topic for magic, so we will look at this a bit closer, not only for your own good, but also for your own deeper understanding for the future: some of you will become teachers and mentors to the next generations, so it pays to understand the issue. It is not really a problem so much as it is a shift in our human consciousness brought about by external change, and we need to adapt.

Until recently, a child growing up would be exposed to books, to inert toys that didn't speak or have screens, and to long hours of boredom. A child, particularly a lone child, would spend hours in imaginary play with their toys, outside in nature, and reading books while visualizing the characters and the action in their heads. Boredom drives the mind to amuse itself and use its imagination to bring books and toys to life. That is why it is so important for children to experience boredom.

Before there was free education for all, many children were illiterate and could not read; but in their communities storytelling was a major feature of their lives, not only for entertainment but also for the passing on of mythic histories and tribal identity.

Children and adults alike would listen to storytellers, and their imaginations would form images of the characters and the action.

It is this same mechanism that comes into play when you read a novel, and then see the film: often the film is disappointing not because of the divergence from the storyline, but because the images on the film are not as good as the ones you formed in your head.

These days children in certain communities develop in a different way. They are placed before a screen/television from being babies, their toys are often computerized in action and voice, and they are constantly looking at screens all day – so many different aspects of their lives are projected outwards in computer games and movies, that the innate imaginary ability does not get as good a work out as it really needed. These are extremes, of course, but it is becoming more prevalent in developed countries, and that will bring with it a change in how children use their imaginations.

An adult who has grown up in such an environment will find it harder to use their imagination, but the brain is clever and can adapt, develop, and focus in the most amazing ways.

Some people have strong visualization skills no matter what they did in childhood, and they will find visionary magic easy. However, if such a strong natural ability is combined with mental health conditions like schizophrenia, then magical visionary work will be impossible. Someone suffering from schizophrenia will have a strong imagination, but it is unfocused. Worst of all, the sufferer often cannot distinguish clearly between reality and fantasy.

The imagination is a complex mechanism that can do a great many different things, and can be used in many different ways. It is a good mechanism for memory: we remember things much better if we visualize them, and it is this use of the imagination that people used, via storytelling, to pass information on down through generations in communities that were illiterate.

The imagination can also be used to talk to deeper layers of ourselves, hence its use in psychology. And it is a mechanism that can be used to project our consciousness, our mind, beyond our body: we are not trapped in our skin. It can also allow other beings, non-physical (spirits, etc.) and physical (anything that is living), to talk with us.

A magician consciously learns and intentionally develops all these mechanisms as part of their foundational skills, and uses them extensively in magic. Where it can go badly wrong is when someone has an illness, disability, or condition that skews these mechanisms. Conditions like schizophrenia, psychosis, and hormone imbalance can affect these natural mechanisms, often to the point that the sufferer is not aware that there is a problem—though everyone else is.

With conditions like schizophrenia and psychosis, the person is often unable to distinguish what is their own voice, what voices in their heads are the result of their condition (i.e. their scrambled imagination), and what voices are from beings outside of them. Often it is a mixture of all three, and their imagination becomes like a constantly bleeding wound. It needs to 'output' all the time, to exteriorize itself constantly, and there is no focus, control, or discernment. The person cannot distinguish what is what or whom, and they become trapped in a nightmare of constant noise and stimuli.

From my own experience of helping and working with people with these mental health issues, I have found that a lot of the time, the output—voices, images, ideas, paranoias—are products of the imagination spiralling out of control. *But*, I have also come across sufferers where a few of the voices they hear are ones I can also hear, where I can perceive a being involved. I do not think the 'being' is the cause of the condition so much as part of the symptomatic picture: the sufferer has no inner boundaries to shut out such beings.

There is nothing you can do about this practically or magically: it is up to the medical profession to help them. However, I did find that when such people were told either to ignore the voices (or images) or to take control and tell them to shut up or go away, then they were more able to cope. Treating each voice as a 'real' entity enabled the sufferer to take control of the situation and make choices. John Forbes Nash Jr. took this approach successfully with his own mental health issues, and his writings on normality, schizophrenia, and evolutionary psychology are very interesting.

Basically, the brain has this wide-ranging mechanism of imagination that can be put to use for many things, magic included, and the key is understanding the various extremes that can present in people. With that understanding, you begin to see how wide ranging the spectrum can be for people in magic, and that as you move away from the centre point of 'absolute normal' in any direction, it comes with gifts and curses. The far extremes of these mechanisms, from one end of the spectrum of 'can't see, can't hear, can't do anything at all with the imagination, to the other end of the spectrum 'see, hear, and live everything all in a jumble', tend to exclude people from magic: if you cannot control and focus the mind and trigger the imagination, you are missing a major skill necessary in magic. But for the most part, magicians are somewhere on the spectrum away from the midpoint of total 'normality', and training, discipline, common sense, and discernment turn that quirk into a real high functioning skill.

The thing to take away from this as a student is that that 'absolute normal' is rarely found in magicians. It is not their quirks that make them magicians: those are more like raw ingredients. Rather it is their focus, training, and operating skills that the quirks can flow through that makes them magicians.

6.7 Advice

Here is some basic practical advice on how to approach visionary work.

1. Don't do visions lying down; it is too easy to drift off to sleep. Deeper into the course there are some visions that are done lying down intentionally, so that you will fall asleep and go into a deeper state of contact. In such cases, the vision becomes a stepping stone for your deeper self. The vision takes you to a place (and triggers the boundary protections), and if/when you need to commune with the contact at a very deep level, you will fall asleep. But this is a rare way of working that is only used in specific ways for very good reason.

2. Always follow the advice in the lesson. Never ignore or circumvent a prescribed action, like tuning and opening gates, lighting candles, or sitting in a particular way. Everything is there for a reason.

3. Always treat what you see in vision as real, unless you start to get things that you know are straight out of your mind, like cartoon characters, movie personalities, or internet game visuals. Treating all imaginative interactions as real, in the early stages of training, breaks down the barriers that our culture has erected in us. Overanalyzing or questioning everything will quickly shut down the bridge of communion with the inner worlds. Once you have become used to working in vision, certain aspects of the vision will begin to solidify and you will start to recognize and feel

what is real and what is just your imagination. Eventually you will learn to filter your imagination out naturally so that your interactions become clear and powerful.

4. Do not use the vision as entertainment, and do not veer from the intended visionary path and vanish into flights of fancy. Too many people follow their curiosity or flights of fancy and end up losing their contact as they play in a pool of their imagination. It takes great discipline and patience to develop the inner 'muscle' for true visionary magic. This is one of the places where the need for self-imposed discipline and boundaries comes in.

5. Keeping a diary of your visions and experiences is important so that you can go back and look at it in years to come. It also helps one to remember the vision, what happened, what contacts were made, and what your responses were. Later, when you come across something in your reading that you saw in vision, your notes will both help confirm this, and help you understand better what you are reading.

6. Finally, prepare properly for visionary work. When you are about to do work, lock doors, unplug or turn off phones, and if other people are in the house, ask them not to disturb you. Have no music playing, and no televisions on nearby.

There is nothing constant in the universe. All ebb and flow, and every shape that's born, bears in its womb the seeds of change.

— *Ovid*

Chapter Seven

The Adversity Of Magical Training

For of all things good and fair, the gods give nothing to man without toil and effort.

— *Prodicus*, The Education of Hercules

Magic, real magic, is tough, hard work and a training that never ends. It is a vast, endless lake of learning, developing, evolving, and strengthening that brings with it the evolution of the personality, the soul, and the world around you. It turns you into an active participant with everything around you, rather than being a passive passenger at the mercy of the Fates. Sure you can buy a few grimoires and utter spells while holding a skull and waving a wand, but that is not the magic we are talking about.

There are many adversities on the path of magical training and magical living. Some are small, some are great; and as you develop you learn more and more coping skills to help you navigate past them. These coping strategies are both inner and outer, and they are also Divine. To balance these struggles, the magical path also gives great and wonderful gifts. It is with the balance of adversity that we can truly appreciate the gifts that come to us, instead of taking them for granted.

Once you are past the Apprentice section you will have a core of basic coping skills for building and strengthening as you progress through the rest of the course, and beyond. The tests never end: they are there to evolve and strengthen you, and to develop your wisdom. Most people who step onto the Apprentice path have little real skill for dealing with adversity, particularly when they come from a culture centred around making life comfortable and easy.

In this chapter we will look only at those adversities and problems that can crop up for an Apprentice, as the methods learned there will be the seeds that will grow into large and long-lived trees of wisdom. We will start with the simplest of adversities, and work our way through to the major hurdles of your training.

Some of what follows has already been covered a little in earlier chapters, but here we will look at things in more depth and breadth. Once you are past the Apprentice training, then what you will have achieved and learned, together with your developing wisdom and your mentor's assistance, will see you through the rest of your training.

First let us look at why certain adversities feature on the magical path, as cultures that have turned them into an enemy have trained people to fear them instead of embracing them as part of the process. We avoid what we fear; and what we avoid, we give up the chance to develop through.

7.1   The function of adversities

Adversities in magical or mystical training are dynamics that have been deeply understood for a long time, and yet recently the understanding of the necessity of adversity has become lost in a world where comfort and the fulfilling of wants is what drives the people. You cannot become a top-class athlete without pain, endurance, disappointment, challenge, and sacrifice. It is not that these adversities are sought after for themselves, i.e. someone who wants to be a top athlete does not purposely seek disappointment, rather it is simply part of the process that matures and strengthens the person.

And so it is with real magical training: you do not actively invite adversity, nor do you wallow in it or take pride in it, rather it is simply a byproduct of the training, but one that cannot be avoided as it is one of the main ingredients that forces the magician back upon themselves. This in turn makes them independent, strong, and mature. It is also through various adversities great and small that we truly come to learn balance not in theory, but in raw physical truth. Every adversity is specific to you, and what it is doing is showing you where imbalance lies, so that it can be rebalanced. You may fight against it, get angry, and at times feel defeated, but if you endure and develop, looking back you will see how each hurdle you overcame was very necessary, and in turn gave you great gifts.

Each person is different, and the adversities that will present are triggered by each magical step you take: whatever is imbalanced, wherever there is a weakness, wherever there is an immaturity, it will be brought to the surface for you to tackle. It can come in the form of outer mundane/practical issues, or in the form of situations/environment, or as inner personal struggles – usually it is all of these and more.

For some, their adversities start from their childhood. Some are born to walk a magical and mystical path, and life will pummel them from the earliest possible time to give them the necessary internal skills, strength, and coping mechanisms for attaining their greatest potential. However, if they do not step up to those experiences as adults and tackle them with as much courage as they can, then they will devolve into victimhood, and their potential path closes down. Many are called; many have potential, but only those who do not give up will get there.

And for those who do not give up, whatever you need will be placed in your path. Trust is a major aspect of mystical magic, as is paying attention. An old saying that my mother used to tell me helped me through much of the adversity of my childhood and young adulthood; and when I was walking the difficult years of my magical growth, it always turned out to be true: "When the door slams shut, turn and look for the window that has been opened for you: you will find it if you look."

Anyone who seeks to develop and evolve on a magical or spiritual path, and is trying to walk that path while developing their balance, will never be allowed to fall. You may stumble many times, and you may have to scale high walls, rivers, and rocky roads—the adversities—but you will always be *upheld in necessity*: what you need will find a way to you, be it food, shelter, etc.

7.2   Simple adversities

The small adversities can present in a myriad of ways, and they present always for purpose: remember, any adversity or difficulty that you experience can teach you something, and also has a functional purpose: it may slow down your studies, or kick you into action. Most of all they are there to teach you the first skills you need in magic: ingenuity, and patience.

When people progress beyond Module I of their Apprentice training, they are exposed to ritual, ritual space, and ritual tools. The first thing that comes to mind for a lot of people is that they need a dedicated space, special altars, shiny tools, and lots of things to buy . Some people are lucky enough to have access to all of that, in which case one of the lessons they will have to learn is that such luxuries can become a trap that limits further development.

Most of us—me included—have no such dedicated space, or special altars or implements. For years I had five white cotton napkins for my altars, and wherever I was working I would lay them on furniture, stools, piles of books, even the cooker and the draining board. You work with what you have. I had little privacy, as I had a hostile husband and two small children. I would work either early in the morning before anyone got up, or wait for an hour alone in the house. At one point, I announced that I needed time to myself for half an hour or an hour, and did not want to be disturbed, and I would go into the bedroom and work. Other times I went outside when I lived near nature spots, and sometimes I had to do an outer ritual in my head, and walk around a space, seemingly just walking and pausing.

For tools I looked in thrift stores. I bought a plain bread knife for a sword, a mug for a vessel, and so forth. These days I have things scattered around my house so they look like ornaments: tools hidden in plain sight. To this day, when a visitor comes to my house, they may find it unusual looking, but they would not see any directional altars or tools, they will only see eccentric ornaments. Even when magicians visit, it often takes them an hour or two of being in the house—which is tiny, so nothing is hidden—before they suddenly smile and nod: they have spotted the pattern hidden in plain sight.

This ingenuity not only teaches you to flex and bend with life while staying within your training parameters, but it also teaches you what is important and what is not. A white tea towel on a cabinet or a pile of books is no different to a solid purpose-made altar with lots of fancy mystical carving. It is the focus, intent, and work that makes an object special, not the object itself. Each cloth I used as an altar I would mark with a tiny letter in the corner, to make sure that I always used it in the same direction: they were the true magical directional altars. I never used them for anything else once they had been used as an altar: they became exclusive for the work.

It is a very important lesson in basic magic to understand that the trappings do not make the magic, you do. The trappings can become a trap, glamour that sucks you in, so that your magic becomes all about the look, the flourish, and the status, and not the actual work. That is the first trap of magic, and the biggest one that many never get beyond. Whole magical lodges are dedicated to trappings, and they are constantly stuck in the first stage of magic without even realizing it.

An adept is one who can, with nothing other than the clothes they stand up in, do magic in its deepest and most powerful forms. An adept is not drawn into traps; he or she sees them and has no desire for them.

7.3 Loneliness

Loneliness is another little adversity that can present at the beginning of a person's magical path. This can either be because of their physical isolation, or because they are surrounded by people who think differently to them. This is something to be endured and recognized, before you step into connections that lift you up. Loneliness first teaches you how different you are from others. Then it teaches you how you may seek connection from outside of yourself, but first you must learn to be at peace with yourself. Such peace cannot be achieved through logic or psychology; it must be achieved by actually being alone. Through enforced isolation, you turn first to yourself, then to the Divine all around you.

Loneliness can appear at any time on your magical path, and it can return in different forms until you truly 'get it.' Its expression also depends on your fate path. You can be alone while surrounded by people, then alone with no day-to-day contact with others. However and whenever loneliness presents, do not despair and do not fight it. Simply be patient. First learn to endure, and then to settle into it. Later, you will learn to relish it. We do not voluntarily withdraw completely, as often the path of a magician is out in the world; rather we learn to accept isolation as sometimes necessary and functional.

Once we learn to accept and be comfortable with a state like loneliness, we have lost the 'want' and have accepted ourselves and the situation as necessary. Once the 'want' has passed and you understand it, then doors will start to open and connections will be made. The process of acquiring a magical family begins, and continues throughout your life. You will cross paths with magical people in the strangest of places, and directly through your training. At Quareia, we are always working hard to try and connect people through social media and gatherings where folks can meet, socialize, and make friends.

Understand that your need to connect with others is about your need to express yourself, or be taken care of, or to have an audience, or to be comforted. Whatever the basis of your want, once you understand it, see it, and recognize it, then it can no longer rule you, your decisions, or your magic. You have spotted part of yourself that could be a weakness, and that awareness will serve you in your development. The endurance will give you strength and patience, and you will never again feel threatened by the prospect of being alone. And as many other serious magicians will tell you, once lessons are learned and you are ready to step forward on your path, you will never feel really alone again.

7.4 Cultural persecution

This can be a serious issue for magicians in some parts of the world, even today. For the most part, your magic is hidden behind closed doors; but sometimes you have to go outside and work in nature or out in the community. This is where a person living in a society hostile to magic has to be careful.

For a student, there are ways around things for most of the tasks in the course. Using a kitchen knife as your sword is not ideal, but it will work. Wandering around looking like a tourist, pretending that you are doing a science experiment, or doing something to help your child with a science experiment, can often be effective disguises.

When even such adaptations will not work, then look carefully at the task you have been set. What is the reason behind it? Is there any way to adapt it to do some of the work physically? If not, then it must be all done in your mind. This is much harder, but it can still trigger what is necessary. Working a ritual completely in vision is not impossible, but it does require mental focus. Sometimes a task may just simply be impossible: in such a case, write down why you cannot do it, and leave the door open for that lesson in case an opportunity arises for you to complete it.

The basic premise is to do whatever you can, no matter how hard it is, and accept the things you cannot do. If you are totally honest with yourself and not just being lazy, then the pattern will work around you. The magical pattern of the course is built around balance and necessity, and what is truly necessary for your training will be made available to you in some way or another. And what is truly not necessary, you will not do. It is individual to the person, and you will find that the powers will work with and around you if you are brutally honest with yourself.

I have worked rituals where the sword needed to be buried briefly, then cast in water. I had to work in a strict Islamic community, and being found doing magic could have meant violence directed at me—or worse. I bought a pendant that was a sword, aligned it with my sword at home—you learn about this in the course—and when it came time to do the work, I sat beside a river, took off my pendant, and quietly stuck it in the ground by my side. After waiting a while, I took out a handkerchief, pulled out the pendant, and slipped it into the cloth. I then pretended to dampen the cloth in the river to wipe my forehead. All the recitations and actions were done in my head or whispered, and once I had finished, I put the pendant back on my chain and slipped it back under my clothing. I did this in full view of others, and simply appeared to sit but the river looking out over the landscape, and at one point dampened a cloth to cool myself.

The problems for someone in a culturally repressive society are not like those faced by someone who simply lives in a big city, where getting to nature is a bit of a struggle. Struggle is good; oppression is not. Never risk getting yourself arrested, and never avoid doing something simply because it is hard work or inconvenient. And learn to think sideways. Many homes have a decorative, cultural, or antique sword or dagger hanging on a wall: there is your magical blade, hiding in plain sight.

If you have to be out in nature for a task and you truly cannot get there, then work in a garden, a friend's garden, a public park, or anywhere with a bit of grass. Figuring out how to do something is all part of the process. Nothing is ever easy in magic, and the difficulty teaches you skills you didn't know you were capable of mastering.

7.5 Lack of money

We covered things like resources in a previous chapter, and how Quareia will help when absolutely necessary; but there is also a dynamic here that can defeat you if you are not aware of it. Most Quareia work can be done without spending much (or any) money, but sometimes you will need to acquire something, and the task cannot be adapted or skipped.

If you truly do not have the resources, and what you need is absolutely necessary, then open the gates and tell the contacts this. By the time you come to need something, you will know how to do this. Also get in contact and ask Quareia.

But in general, people who think they have no resources are in fact pretty well resourced: it is about choice. No inner contact—or Quareia—will help you if you simply choose not to use a resource you have. If you eat out, buy coffees while going to work, can choose not to work, or pay to get your nails done, then you have resources. It is amazing how many people think they are broke who are not, particularly in first world countries. You need to look carefully at yourself, weigh your life against necessity, and decide how important the magical path is to you. When you are truly without, the universe will step up and help you, if you are true to yourself and your path.

> Adversity has the effect of eliciting talents, which in
> prosperous circumstances would have lain dormant.
>
> — *Horace (65 B.C.–8 B.C.)*

7.6   Complex adversities

The two most prominent powers that run through the Apprentice section are what I call the Grindstone and the Unraveller. These powers are thoroughly discussed in the course, but let us look here at how they actually manifest in the life of a student. This will give you far more understanding of what is happening to you as you train. The effects of these powers—and they are indeed *conscious* powers—start from the moment you begin training, and they will stay with you for the rest of your life. In the early days of your training, they will be tough taskmasters, but as you evolve and develop they will become your greatest 'wingmen' in magic and in your life. They are life's greatest trainers.

Think about an Olympic athlete or a military Marine. When they first start training, their trainers are tough, uncompromising, and completely focused on pushing the recruit to their limits. Later, these trainers become guides, upholders, and advisors who help the athlete or soldier attain their best, while holding them within the network of support. So it is with magical training.

But why does it have to be so difficult? True magical training will only be as difficult as it needs to be for each individual. The more baggage we carry, the more has to be seen, understood, and shed before we can truly move forward; and the weaker our muscles, the more training is needed to strengthen them. Humans are pretty lazy: if we are not pushed then we will often just float around happily until something upsets our stasis. This is not true only of humans: need drives action in every creature, and in every cell in our bodies.

Stepping onto the path of magical training means undergoing a series of little deaths until everything useless has been taken away and composted. We are left stripped, exposed, and battered, but lightened of many loads and ready to start the process of rebuilding.

So what are these loads that need stripping? It varies from person to person, and they are presented and taken off layer by layer. One of the first major layers presented for removal is abundance. This can be easy for some and difficult for others. In the USA, for example, some religions and spiritual paths seek to convince people that abundance is good, that you deserve it, and that it is a sign that God loves you. This is a marketing ploy which plays to our evolutionary 'squirrel' mechanism discussed earlier. Behind such marketing ploys are products, mega-churches, and con men.

But in the west, and particularly the USA, the population has been trained to think that more is better. On a magical path, such thinking becomes a problem, as magic must be driven by necessity if it is to be balanced and successful. So one the first steps in magical training is to learn to look around you and what you have. You are encouraged to clear out your cupboards and wardrobes, take out whatever you do not use, and give them away. Suddenly that coat that has hung there for three years without use is taken out of stasis and put where it is necessary: you give it to a shelter, charity, a homeless person on the street, or someone you know who needs a coat. This changes the energy dynamics around you: you become part of the pattern of *necessity*. How you can you possibly expect a being or spirit to help you when you sit on unused resources while others go without?

This action triggers the Unraveller power: the hoarding mechanism is slowly unravelled from you until you start to realize that everything you do (and *are*) in life is affected by magic, and that life *is* magical. You let go of what you do not need so that it can go to those who do need it. What you need will then start to make its way to you. If you are doing what you should be doing, then what you need will find its way to you. This simple dynamic becomes powerful indeed on the magical path, and the first step is to let go of excess. Do you really need your watch to be a Rolex whose price could feed a family for a year? Or do you just need to watch to keep time?

For some, the changes brought by the training will be massive; for others they will be small and simple. It all depends on what state your life is in.

As the power flow is Ma'at, the other side of the coin can also happen: if you are without and struggling, then what you need in true necessity will be put in your path. If you are in a bad place, location, or situation and are trying to get free, and it is necessary for your fate to be free of it, then the power will open doors for you to move forward. All this depends on your willingness to walk the path in truth and integrity. And it is a long process: it doesn't happen all at once, but unfolds as and when it is necessary, at a pace you can truly cope with—though this is often not a pace you would prefer!

There is a saying in the Qur'an, 'God does not burden any human being with more than he is well able to bear. Allah, the Most High, Speaks the truth.' (Surah 2:285-6.) This saying has a lot of magical knowledge within it. When you walk on the mystical and magical path, you are never given a burden you cannot truly cope with. And when you truly reach your limit and utter it, then you have then found your limitation. Knowing the limits of what you can cope with is important, and once you reach your limit in some situation and understand it, then the pressure backs off and necessity flows to you.

That does not mean you are never given burdens; in fact the reverse is true. The deeper in a mystical magical path you go, the harder your work and life gets; yet greater also are the necessary gifts placed in your path. The problem, most of the time, is that we do not realize how strong we really can be, how much grit we actually have, and how our perseverance can make us strong, stable, and balanced people. This strengthening process, as I have said before in this guide, is the 'gym for the soul.' To work with real power in magic, you have to be as strong and as balanced as possible.

It is also wise to understand that a great deal of our adversities—not all of them—come from our own actions and choices. This is why in the Apprentice section you learn a lot about cause and effect in magic and in life, a subject that has truly fallen by the wayside in modern magical training.

> To accuse others for one's own misfortunes is a sign of want
> of education. To accuse oneself shows that one's education
> has begun. To accuse neither oneself nor others shows that
> one's education is complete.
>
> — *Epictetus* (A.D. 55–135)

Once you have examined the surface layers of 'abundance' in your life, then your training starts to dig deeper. What is out of balance in your body? If how you tend to your body is out of balance, or your body itself has become toxic, weak, or imbalanced, then your health will be next on the agenda. It is pretty common in one's early classical magical training to have illnesses crop up or come to light, and they can be harsh ones that bash you. This is not a punishment or a test of endurance; rather it is to force you to look at how you care for your body, to be aware of your toxic eating habits, or of toxic behaviour that will ultimately poison you if it continues. Once magic is triggered in your body, then your body will start to respond by showing you where it is struggling.

This also changes your relationship with your body, and also changes your understanding of your own body. You will begin to learn its unique strengths and weaknesses, and what you can really cope with, and what you cannot. Some people have a tough time with this; for others it is not such a big deal. It all depends on what state your body is in, what your attitude is towards it, and whether that attitude is right or not. Some people merely have to change their diet: through magic, they start to react to certain foods which start to make them feel ill or toxic. But for me it was a tough road.

When I wrote the Apprentice section, I was also doing the work, not only to revisit it, but also to observe it from a different angle to evolve and 'better' that work. So I went through every single process in the course, in the short time of three years. That was truly the toughest thing I have ever done in my life—and I have done some pretty tough things. I was also going through an accelerated menopause as I wrote the course, and the way I had learned to look after my body was now no longer applicable. I had to find another way, and I was bashed until I learned.

Lastly, some of the adversities which will undoubtedly trigger are mythic ones. This is why you were encouraged to read mythic tales and mystical legends. They are key adversities that will mark your progress on the path, and will bring about magical change within you. The mythic patterns that trigger will vary from person to person: it will depend, among other things, on your history, ancestral bloodlines, and culture.

For example, there is a lot of Egyptian mythology and mystical magic in this course, and one myth in particular triggered for me intensely when I came to writing that part of the course. There were two physical manifestations in rapid succession. The first was an attack of shingles in my left eye, which caused great pain, a fixed pupil, and loss of sight. I kept writing regardless. All it did was slow me down a little, and at first I did not get the magical message. Then, shortly after, I was working in the garden cutting things back, and a thorn flew into my left eye and embedded itself in my eyeball.

I visited the hospital again to get my eye checked, and once again, I experienced a loss of sight, pain, and a slow recovery. Only in that second recovery did I realize that I was manifesting the injured Eye of Horus—the left eye—which is explored briefly in the course and which I was working on at the time.

So I went back and explored the myth and the magical dynamics of the Eye of Horus, and realized that I was manifesting the magical dynamic. My sight and the 'casting of my glance' with the left eye was being changed. And change it did. My physical sight in my left eye is now changed permanently, but the inner magical aspect of the left eye dynamic was also changed, for the good. Through knowing the mythic pattern of the Eye of Horus, I came to understand why those incidents happened, and I learned how to work with the magical gift I had been given. That is how magical adversity works.

7.7 A challenge to preconceptions

Another dynamic that kicks in is having your preconceptions and prejudices challenged. One thing to remember in all this is that magic transforms you to help you *evolve*. If your magical training is focused on yourself, on improving yourself, then it will not happen, and in fact the reverse is likely to happen. (Some magical training systems really do not understand this dynamic.) The change *within* comes from your work casting *outwards*, in service. I have talked about this a lot before, as it is so important.

As you work outwards, first in connection, then in service, you start to change within. As each layer surfaces, it challenges you with exterior and interior events. The layer of us that houses our prejudices, preconceptions, and thoughtlessness starts to make itself known once the more superficial challenges have been met.

We all have preconceived ideas about things. Usually they are incorrect and fed by our prejudice. Prejudice is a defence and survival mechanism deeply embedded in our psyche. Its aim is to bond a small community together so that it stays safe. But in the world we now live in, this mechanism serves only to devolve us and cut us off from each other.

Prejudice comes from not knowing, not understanding, and from deeply fearing *the other*. It is fed by a lack of wider education, by a lack of opportunity to mix, and by a lack of ability to step into the shoes of others. Base human dynamics like this have no place in magic, and particularly not in Quareia magic. To step into the deeper magical Mysteries, we have to leave such base instincts behind, and step into a way of thinking rooted in Ma'at and necessity.

It is vitally important in magic to know why things happen; why beings, people, and creatures behave a certain way; and to distinguish between rejecting a person or community because of their colour, culture, religion, appearance, or sexuality, and rejecting them because they are unbalanced, violent, or inherently degenerate. Every community in the world has a group it defines as *the other*, some minority within it that it believes must be 'kept down.' Often the *other* group is poorly educated and/or poorly resourced, and various differences will keep it apart from the surrounding community. And yet within that group there will be good and bad, bright and stupid, healthy and diseased, nasty and nice. We are all human, and every group, *without exception*, has its good and bad members.

If you turn your back on a whole group of people, then that is an imbalanced and unjust action, as you are also turning your back on the good people, the honest people, the bright people: this breaks the laws of Ma'at. It is up to the magician, as they develop, to look beyond their base instincts and to judge each individual on their own merits. There are killers, extremists, and rapists in 'rich' and 'good' communities just as there are in 'bad' communities.

Excluding people who are unjust, violent, or very racist can be a balanced exclusion, but it depends on what your role is in life. If you are a doctor, a lawyer, a mediator—someone duty-bound to help others regardless of their beliefs and behaviours—then such an exclusion is unbalanced and unjust. If, however, you are trying to build, evolve, and create in your work, then whom you exclude should be decided individual by individual, based on the person's long-term inherent behaviour towards others. You should not be excluding people simply because they are members of some group such as a race, religion, or sexuality. Exposure to different people with different ideas brings growth. Even if you do not agree with them, they will expose you to different viewpoints, which will expand your awareness and knowledge.

It is vitally important in magical development not to beat yourself up if you find, on self-examination, that you do harbour some prejudice. Rather it is a matter of learning to step back from your old beliefs and examine them in the cold light of day. What is their root? Where did those ideas come from? Do they have real merit? How do they affect your development? What behaviour in others triggers your prejudice? Where do those behaviours come from—what causes them? This will start you on a journey not only of self-discovery, but also of learning about other people, what makes them tick, and why they are as they are.

This in turn teaches you how to analyse, which is a major skill in magic: through visionary and contacted work, you will come across many different types of inner beings, and through being able to analyse their behaviour/presentation, you will learn how to communicate properly, how to assess the value of your work, and most importantly, how to not let preconceived ideas steer your work. Magic is true exploration, and learning how to step forward with common sense and logic as opposed to emotive reactions will put you in a strong position upon your magical path.

Let's just spend some time looking at the root causes of 'difference' and those behaviours that can trigger prejudice. For some, particularly those students who have travelled a lot or have been exposed to many different cultures from childhood, the following comments will be obvious. But for others, particularly those who have not travelled much outside their own country other than for holidays, the following comments may trigger deeper thought, analysis, and understanding.

7.8   Crime and disease

Many minority groups in different countries have fled war, poverty, disease, and oppression. Some have ended up in a foreign country through slavery, and the deep history of their oppression continues to define their present day community. Such minority communities are often plagued by high crime, poverty, and disease. Poverty and oppression are fuel to the fire of crime, and where there is a lot of poverty, there will also be crime.

It is easy to say, "oh, this minority community are a bunch of thieves and thugs," but when you are in long-term poverty and cannot feed or clothe your children properly, theft can be part of your existence. I have lived in minority communities that had serious poverty, and I realized that while high ideals are great when you have a full stomach, when you have nothing, you fight to survive.

It is also easy, as a well-fed and housed person, to cast judgement and talk about choices, and to imagine what in such a situation you would do to make it better. *Never judge until you, too, have lived for a good length of time in such conditions.* Poverty, disempowerment, and oppression destroy the depths of a person, and you cannot stand in judgement until you have walked in their shoes.

Lack of education

In minority and poor communities, the chance of getting a decent education is often nonexistent. Without a good solid education, rising out of poverty can be difficult, if not impossible. Not everyone is bright and able to pull themselves out of a poverty cycle without help. And a lack of education in a poor and/or minority community can be a breeding ground for extremism, whatever their religion or culture. It is the root of poverty, oppression, and violence. When you are oppressed and have no education, then you have no way to express or understand why that oppression is happening: your only way to fight back is through violence and aggression. When you have an education, you have a voice and you know how to use it. This is one of the reasons that governments with authoritarian leanings tend to advocate policies that strip schools and universities of funding: it takes them out of the reach of the poor. If the bottom layer of society cannot voice its discontent, then it cannot overthrow the regime. It will simply become a violent layer of society, which can then be used as an excuse for more oppressive policies.

Appearing different

Minority cultures that appear different because of their clothing are often attacked, maligned, and feared. Usually this is due to a lack of understanding, and the inherent human drive to favour conformity. Currently in the west, Muslim women wearing the hijab is a major driver of racist and violent attacks on the streets. So let us use the hijab as an example.

Different cultures develop different ways of dressing, at first due to climate, health, and environmental necessity. Ever tried wandering around in the desert in full sun, or avoiding head lice without a head covering? These dress codes of necessity become status symbols: if you work in the fields as a peasant, you cannot be wearing layers of fabric that are going to get in your way. So a woman wearing layers of silk is stating that she does not have to work in the fields, therefore she is from a wealthy family. Her skin will be fairer as it will be exposed less to the sun. Thus her light skin and her veil are status symbols of wealth and privilege. The veil as a female status symbol is first mentioned in history in the Assyrian sumptuary laws (Middle Assyrian 1114–1076 B.C.) though there are carvings of veiled women dating from around 2500 B.C.. So the veil has deep and ancient roots in the cultures of the Near and Middle East.

Later, the pecking order of society asserts itself further through religion. If the woman is covered, then not only is she from a wealthy family, but she is also from a 'good and modest' family. The veils start to become not only symbols of wealth and status, but also of religious and moral standing. The politics of Islam and the West have further intensified in the last twenty years, and in many countries the hijab has become a political football as a result.

But a woman who walks down the street in the West wearing the hijab is dressing in a way that has been normal in her culture for thousands of years. Who has the right to tell her to stop? Why should a person be feared or reviled simply because they are dressing normally for their own family, culture, and religion? People in the West may say, "when in the West, do as we do." This is the age-old instinct that associates conformity with security: recognize it for what it is. Understand where the hijab comes from and what it means to the wearer, then examine the negative reactions to it without emotion.

So how does prejudice become a magical adversity in training? Magic is about connections, conversations, bridging, mediating, opening, and closing. To operate in any real depth a true adept, you need to work these dynamics on a deep level, and any imbalance or baggage of yours will affect that work. You cannot in truth get rid of all your baggage and imbalances, but you can get them right down to the minimum, and govern them with logic and necessity. That way, your emotional and instinctive patterns of behaviour—your prejudices—can be transformed into an early warning system as opposed to a blockage.

By examining and challenging your preconceived ideas, and exploring the background, root, and reasoning behind different behaviours, you learn to apply logic and understanding. This starts to change you, first on the surface, then deeper at an inner level. It prepares you for all the different sorts of inner contact that you will have, and to respond to those contacts on their own merits rather than by your preconceived notions or prejudices. This is particularly important for magicians who have grown up as Jews, Christians, or Muslims, as the polarized view of good and evil in the three Abrahamic religions will be a filter through which you view inner contacts. Inner contact and inner beings are not grouped into nice identifiable bundles of 'angels' and 'demons,' so it is important, and especially so when you become Adept, to be prepared to see into the depths of a situation or contact, and use logic to assess its merits. Your subconscious, then your inner self, will start to shift from its tribal affiliation with what is familiar to what is necessary for balance.

Being prejudiced is as unbalanced and unhealthy as being 'all accepting,' which is the other end of the scale. The more you work on your preconceived ideas and dig for their reasoning and logic, the more you will develop as a bridge that allows communication with any 'being' that is necessary, and that blocks whatever is unbalanced and unnecessary. So you begin to see how important it is to move away from your cultural programming and towards logical thought, so that you mind can start to learn flexibility. (As an aside, it also teaches you to look beyond the surface appearance of a thing, which is extremely important in magic.)

Adversity is the first path to truth.

— *Lord Byron* (A.D. *1788–1824)*

7.9 Gender and identity

Gender and sexuality can be a major issue for people going into magic, as a lot of magic, particularly western magic, is seemingly geared towards the white straight male. The overall structure of many western magical schools is one that was put in place during the late 19th century where the world and people were viewed through a very polarized lens: white and not white, male and female, good and bad. A gay man was considered an abomination, and a woman doing anything other than producing babies and running households was scandalous. If you were not white Anglo Saxon then you were considered inferior.

To give the magical schools at the time some credit, they tried hard to step away from such closed mentalities, but the aroma of discrimination still lingered. A lot of that fixed mentality still exists in the world of magical training, and it is important for students to be aware of it so they can look out for each other. They must know that such attitudes are not okay, and are not a part of magic.

In terms of gender identity, if a student is fluid with their gender identity, then they should approach their magical work with the same fluidity. However, in general you should not be approaching your magic in terms of your sexual identity, but in terms of what each of your individual magical workings *needs*. Magic is always rooted in necessity, and each magical act should be approached as an individual unit of action. What does *this* pattern need to function? How do I fit within it?

A lot of magic works from you as an individual, so it really does not matter what gender you are or how you identify. You just plug in and get to work. Issues can arise, however, when a magical pattern, usually in ritual, involves polarity power dynamics. It is important for all magicians to learn how to work with polarized power, even if you as an individual are anything but polarized.

The key is to approach each such working individually and decide for yourself where you fit in the pattern and polarity of that particular working. If you are gender fluid, or have a complex gender identity, then you are far luckier than most: you will be flexible enough to fit anywhere on the pattern according to its needs and the intention of the magic. Just remember that each magical working is different, even if it appears superficially the same as a previous one. Don't take anything for granted, and be flexible with how you approach the work.

Gender fluidity has not been much explored in Western magic, so if you are a Quareia student and your gender or sexual identity is complex or not polarized, then take notes. Keep records of your workings, their effects, and so forth. Your experiences and development will help the next generation, and if you make it through the Adept training and become a mentor then you will be invaluable to the next generation not only as a mentor those going through the same identity development, but also in educating those who have no knowledge, understanding, or experience of such issues.

Women and gender is still, sadly a major issue in magic. We women in magic still have to work twice as hard to get any sort of respect, and in some areas of magic we are still relegated to a pseudo-sexual role, for instance as a 'Scarlet Woman,' which is nothing more than a male sexual fantasy.

In Quareia there are no gender defined roles, as in classical magic there are no such things. Polarity workings form a small part of the more advanced work, but they are not as gender defined as they appear, and their purpose is to force the magician to think beyond the stereotypes and to work out, in each particular working, whether they are outputting or receiving energy. This can change from working to working depending on how the person and their body are functioning at the time, and what the flow of energy is: what it is doing and where it is going.

The advice I would give to women is this: do not allow anyone to sideline your work simply because you are a woman, and do not allow any magical group, lodge, or school to keep you down or relegate you to a role simply because of your gender. Ability and hard work is everything in magic, not gender; and I can say that as a postmenopausal woman who has excelled in her field of magic.

When a woman hits menopause (as I did, at high speed) her power does change. It goes through a flux for a few short years, but if you understand not to try and hold on to what you were before menopause, but step forward into a new and often quite different pattern of working, then you will do just fine. Your power and skill set shifts, and it is important not to fight to stay as you were, but to step forward with the understanding that you are morphing into something far more profound. The changes menopause brings to your magic are wonderful: your magic becomes deeper and far more mystical, and once you are over the two or three years of feeling like a madwoman—swinging hormones can do that to you—then you will find a level of stillness that you did not have before. As a female magician I can say that now, on the other side of menopause, is the best time of my magical life.

7.10   The Challenge of the Gods

Once you have divested yourself of things holding you back, the way adversity comes at you changes. It can often present when something is wrong: you may have taken a wrong turn in your life or magical work, or you may need to change but are clinging to a mentality of 'keep on the same path of action, don't keep changing.' Such a mentality comes from the need for security, which is often drilled into people from a young age. But magic is all about change, constant change, and development.

When my energy levels suddenly dip right down, or everything I try to do is blocked or unworkable, I step back and look at what I am doing in every aspect of my life, why I am doing it, and where it could potentially lead. Once I have done as much thinking as I can muster, I will then use divination to see if the blockage, loss of energy, or adversity is there to hold me back for my own good, or whether something I am doing is blocking off my future path.

Often our present actions—or lack of action—can close down future fate patterns. That closing down will drag on your energy or cause everything around you to become unworkable. Often the culprit of the energy drain is a simple little thing, akin to a grain of sand grinding away in your shoe, eventually giving you blisters. Use divination to see what you are doing, or not doing, that is affecting your future fate pattern. When you go off course in a way that affects your future, your energy will really start to drag on you, to force you to step back into the stream of fate and time that will lead you to your greatest potential.

Now you will begin to see why divination is such an important tool in magic, as it helps you navigate these challenges and bring in necessary change. These adversities are there as warnings, so once you are past the first half of your Apprentice training and you suspect that one of these warning adversities has activated, use divination to figure out what is happening. First get an overview of where your path is taking you with the Landscape layout; then use a simple Tree of Life layout to ask if you are indeed on the right path in everything that you do. If you are not, then it will show in the last card.

You then have to look at where the adversity is striking. Is it your health or energy? Or is it your work? Your family? Something else? Finding the root cause of the adversity is not easy and can take some time, but often inspiration will come from the readings, or dreams will highlight the problem for you if it is getting important enough. Pay attention, dodge the bullets, and make the necessary changes. Never get to thinking that you must not make changes: magic itself triggers change. Make changes when they are necessary, and hold your course steady in a storm when that is necessary.

To summarize, we all approach adversity in different ways, and it is important for you to find your own coping mechanisms, and to meet each challenge with a brave heart and a clear mind. My method is to expect and plan for plague, then celebrate when it is simply a cold. Your approach may be different. Find out what works for you. As you are challenged more and more, your coping mechanisms will develop and mature if you do not run away from difficulties, but step up to them and treat each one as a chance for development and learning.

When you fail to overcome an obstacle in your path, pick yourself up, dust yourself off, learn whatever you need to from the experience, and be truthful with yourself. Then step out again with more determination. The more you engage with obstacles that block your path and solve the problems or dodge around them, the stronger and wiser you will get. If you run away or give in, the same obstacle will keep coming back in different guises until you get the message.

The more you learn from adversities, the less harsh and more subtle the adversities will eventually become. You will increasingly pay attention to what may lie ahead (divination is a good tool) and find the path at each crossroads which bears the best fruit for you. The magical pattern will increasingly fit itself more perfectly to you, ensuring that you have exactly what you need, and removing what you do not.

A real adept has generally been through many adversities and learned many lessons, and has extracted knowledge and wisdom from each one. When they stand before you their adepthood is revealed in their eyes and their actions, not by a certificate on their wall or a fancy badge on their lapel. Life is one of the major trainers in magic, so engage with it in all its dysfunctional glory!

March on. Do not tarry. To go forward is to move toward perfection. March on, and fear not the thorns, or the sharp stones on life's path.

— *Kahlil Gibran* (A.D. *1883–1931*)

Chapter Eight

Religions

Beware of confining yourself to a particular belief and denying all else, for much good would elude you—indeed, the knowledge of reality would elude you. Be in yourself a matter for all forms of belief, for God is too vast and tremendous to be restricted to one belief rather than another.

— *Shayhk Myhyi al-Din Ibn al-Arabi*

Since writing the course I have been getting a lot of questions about religion, and especially about what religion a magician should be, and whether you can still do the course while practising certain ones. Because religion can so strongly influence both individuals and cultures, I think it would be useful for people to have a better overview of how religions can intersect with magic, and in particular with Quareia's magic. If you have no religion, or have left behind a religious family, then then this chapter will give you insight into various workings within the course, why they are there, and how to approach them.

The foundation and basis of Quareia training is that it covers knowledge, skills and techniques that are not specific to any particular system, but are often found in many different magical systems: it gets to the core of magic without being hobbled by one specific religious pattern. Most magical systems today have one religion at its core – it is usually because that system grew out of a group of people who were all from one religion, which in turn was the overarching religion of that country/culture. But why does religion appear in magic at all?

To answer that question, you have to step back from the religious mindset—which is harder than it sounds—and look from the outside in. What actually *is* a religion? A religion is a cultural framework that provides a method for communicating and connecting with the Divine. Its dogmas and rules are often rooted in the culture it grew from, and they generally include whatever civil traditions are necessary for a harmonious community.

Before the twentieth century, most countries generally had one overarching religion dominating their culture, though they may also have had some minority religions brought in by immigration. Even in secular countries today there is generally one especially prominent religion that has a defined influence on how the culture works, what laws are enacted, and what the social norms are.

In magic the same happens, even today. There is often an overarching religious pattern at the bedrock of a magical system (though parts of other religions may also be included to add spice). This limits the scope of the system's magic and its inner contact, and it can entrench in the system any latent suppressions or imbalances that run through the religion or the system's magicians.

However, in any magic that reaches beyond petty spells and role playing, there is a strong presence of the Divine. In magic you are working with the powers of the universe, the consciousness of creation. As such, you bump up against the Divine pretty early on. The key is to understand that the Divine—God, Allah, the Unknowable One—is not religious: the Divine and religion are two different things. Religion is man-made, and as such has all the flaws and weaknesses of humans. Divine consciousness, on the other hand, is all around us and within us, regardless of our religion and regardless of humanity. When we eventually become extinct as a species, the Divine will continue, but our religions will not.

8.1   Why does a magician need to learn about religions?

This is the most common question I get from Quareia students, and though this is discussed briefly in the course, people tend to glaze over it or miss it. So an in-depth answer here would probably be useful.

As a magician, you do not work in isolation. You are surrounded by people and communities, and a lot of your magic, both as a student and as an adept, will be about service and helping. You cannot help someone or something (a landmass, for example), if you do not understand the deeper workings behind a religion that is prominent in a culture, or understand where and why things go wrong within a religion, and how that affects everything around them. When a person goes to see a doctor, the doctor will ask about their symptoms, but he will also ask (depending on the issue) about their diet, their job, and so forth. Getting a wider perspective gives the doctor clues about what could be causing their patient's problem, and also what could limit their recovery.

As a magician, you will cross paths with people from all different sorts of religions and cultures who will ask for your help. If you understand their deeper religious mindsets or childhood religious influences, then you will get a wider picture of their story, and also of the method to resolve their problem.

The other, and I feel more important, reason for a serious magician to learn about different religions, is that it shows them the magical commonalities and mystical similarities between various religions, and how those mystical and magical concepts eventually became religious dogmas. The course looks at this in many different ways, sometimes directly, and sometimes with a focus that crosses paths with religious thought.

Once you are able to step back and look at different religions and how they developed—and if you can look without prejudice—then you notice how many times an ancient religious or magical practice is co-opted by a newer religion. Magic was an integral part of ancient religions: the separation between religion and magic only really began with the rise of monotheism.

8.2 Understanding the evolution of religion

To understand magic as it exists in religions, you have to understand how the function of religion has changed over the millennia. In ancient cultures, magical practices were part of the religious duties of the priesthoods (male and female). Ancient religions were greatly concerned with subduing certain powers, keeping other powers happy, and talking to the Divine on behalf of the people. The unwashed masses were not allowed anywhere near the inner parts of the temples, and religious rituals were generally conducted for the deities, and done behind closed doors.

The deities were considered the children of the creator: different expressions of the Divine. They were looked after day and night. A lot of ancient ritual had to do with keeping all the plates spinning to achieve balance and subdue chaos. In the Ancient Egyptian religion, the monarch and elite priesthood were expected to adhere to a code of balance and justice themselves, so that they would be part of the balance and not a cause of chaos.

This created a social order that flowed from the religious structure, which in turn, became a defining feature of the culture. Everything was enmeshed, and when it all went wrong, the finger of blame would be pointed at the Monarch, then the priesthood, and finally the people.

As with all human organizations, in every religion that develops, a power grab eventually happens. Temples would fight each other for supremacy over wealth and resources, and the whole thing would begin to rot and fall apart. Power grabs happen in different ways in different religions, but it happens in all of them, without fail. Power grabs often appear as factionalism at first, with one group accusing another of heresy. But lurking behind this is simply the wish to be on top.

In the Christian church, the Mass, or Eucharist, was originally a ritual performed for God and humanity as a whole, not for the local people. The priest would face the altar with his back to the people, and often there was even a rood screen to block their view, so they could only hear what was happening. Later, some Christian factions did away with most of their rituals and turned churchgoing into a weekly social lecture and prayer session. Finally, in the twentieth century, even the Catholic church turned their priests around, got rid of the altar rails and rood screens, and made Mass much more of an interactive social event.

Of course I am generalizing here, and skipping across the surface of a complex story about how human interaction with the Divine has evolved, but an in-depth lecture is not necessary here. The point is that all religions have a lot in common when it comes to how they were structured, how they evolved, and what their purpose was. Knowing that, and stepping away from any degenerate, ingrained belief in 'one true way' can help a magician enormously, as it allows them to see through a religion's dogma to the inherent patterns that underpin it. This allows the magician to spot the religion's magical aspects (they all have them) and especially any magical patterns taken from earlier systems that have been inserted into the newer religion with a few changes to make them fit.

It is those magical patterns that you learn in Quareia, through study and comparison, and through practice. You cannot fully understand any magical or mystical pattern before you have actually worked within an aspect of it. Studying alone will not allow the Deeper Mysteries of a pattern to surface in your mind. So let us look at how that is approached.

8.3   Working with different religious patterns in Quareia

In your Quareia training you will come across workings that connect you to the Divine without a religion dressing, where there is a simple communion between yourself and the Universal Divine. Later you will work with exercises anchored in a specific religion, so that you get the 'inner' aspect learning of what can flow through that religion, for good and bad. Often these are exercises that you have to repeat, so that you can learn how connections develop over time, what they bring to you for good and bad, and where their magical roots lie.

You are also given exercises that can trigger some of the issues that can flow through a religious pattern, so that you can experience them firsthand. You are not warned about what could happen: personal experience is always the best teacher. And of course everyone is different, and will have different experiences.

In the Adept section, you work with an ancient state religion's pattern that has magic closely enmeshed within it, so that you can have certain extremely direct evolutionary experiences. Here the pattern is used as a vehicle for the adept transformational Justification process.

You will also study a lot of different religious texts, exploring their magical and mystical aspects while looking at where their ideas came from, and how they have evolved over time.

Though only a few religious patterns are worked with directly, the workings themselves will teach you how to approach any religious pattern to learn from it, so that you can, if you wish to, explore other religions using the same methods.

I use the rule of absolutes to get you used to the 'operate from within' method: you are placed within a mystical, magical, or spiritual mindset and structure, and trained to operate an aspect of magic from within that mindset. Sometimes you are not told why, or how long you will be in that structure, or indeed if you will ever be pulled back from it. This enables you to focus your consciousness fully in the pattern.

When you are finally pulled out of a religious or magical pattern and introduced to the next one, you will have gained a much deeper experience of it by working within it, and you will understand better its pitfalls, benefits, beings, issues, and patterns.

When we study magic, we tend to think of that magic within our own cultural and social mindset. That affects how we project that magic outward in our work, service, and action. However, we live in an ever-shrinking world, and we are constantly bumping up against different cultures, religions, and systems. We therefore must be able to confront our biases towards or against many different religions. A true adept not only understands all these different systems, but they can also operate briefly and respectfully from within them as and when necessary in order to achieve something. Healing, exorcism, construction... all these tasks, and many others, require you to understand fully any religious, magical, or cultural systems that may be in play.

To this end, the Quareia student has to be immersed in different religions and magical systems, not to become part of them, but to be informed and to understand them. The working knowledge you gain as a result makes you useful, and it also, as a byproduct, helps you gain a deeper understanding of the sort of issues that can arise within a system or religion. It also helps you spot the many areas of degeneration, imbalance, and sometimes just sheer madness that often develop within such systems during certain periods of history.

So while the actual mechanics of magic that you learn in Quareia are free of any religious or magical systems, you still have to dip into them as a focus or subject matter, and sometimes briefly immerse yourself in them, while also maintaining detached observation, in order to become a knowledgeable, well-rounded adept. This in turn will also, by the time you get to adept level study, lead you to question what is divinity, what is religion, what is magic, what does it mean to you, and how do you either develop your own unique interface with these various energetic structures, or how do you tear such concepts apart and find new evolved expressions.

I also put initiates and adepts in situations where they step over the line from magical work with deities into a more religious, priestly role of tending to a deity. Approaching a deity as a magician is very different from approaching a deity as a devotee; yet often people do not realize there is a difference, or why there is a difference. Rather than just explain it, which is how the apprentices are exposed to this difference, an initiate and adept crosses that line for a while, then steps back. Over the course of a few months, they learn their lessons by direct, practical experience. After that, they can choose from a place of gnosis whether they wish to be a priest or devotee of some aspect of Divinity as well as a magician, and they will *know* the difference between the two roles.

8.4 Dogmas and dangers

Although we tend to associate dogmas with religion, they also crop up in magic, and you will find as you get deeper into the course, that there are many parallels between religion and magic (as they grew up together), and understanding one helps you understand the other.

The dictionary definition of dogma is 'a principle or set of principles laid down by an authority as incontrovertibly true.' Dogmas are created and used to lay down norms of behaviour and to pin down modes of belief that cannot be questioned (unless you are a heretic). Dogmas can be insidious, and can shift the mindset of a large number of people in a particular direction that is accepted as 'the way things are.'

Dogmas are rarely constructed in completion; usually dogmas build slowly, with each layer being added by different 'voices of authority' to tighten the belief structure. We see this in the beginnings of Christianity, from the development of Jesus from 'Christ the Messiah' or prophet, to 'Christ the God'. When we study the gospels, you can see the development between the first gospel (Mark, approx. A.D. 70), and the final gospel of John (approx. A.D. 100) which was not part of the synoptic tradition, where there is the first mention of the divinity of Jesus. It is also worth mentioning here that at that time, it was not unknown for a very special leader to also be called a god—the Roman Emperor being a good example.

Fast forward two hundred years, and Christianity is no longer a Jewish sect closed to Gentiles, but a whole new religion complete with a hierarchy of priesthoods. At the First Council of Nicaea (A.D. 325), the Church's religious leaders met to debate and draw up the specifics of their dogma. Later councils added to this 'creed' of belief, until there was a fully-functioning dogmatic structure that could not be questioned.

If you are interested in teaching or forming a new magical school or pattern in the future, then it is important to understand, while you are a student, how these dogmatic constructs are formed, as they can also occur in magical structures, and to a lesser extent in cultural ones.

Dogmas in magical lines tend to appear when the initial power of formation of the magical line is fading, and that fading tends to happen when people start to bring their agendas to the line. A dogma is about control of thought, the suppressing of questions, and the blocking of individual paths. When a student is in the 'learning phase', often absolutes are used as boundaries so that learning can happen and evolve within a set of parameters. But beyond that learning phase once the absolutes have been dispensed with, the individual's relationship with the Divine and with magic, is unique to that person based upon their experiences. So it is important to fully understand the differences between training absolutes which flex, change and then vanish as the student develops, and magical dogma which is unchanging and cannot be challenged.

But when a trained magician develops their own personal understanding through direct experience, two things can sometimes go wrong: their lodge seeks to reassert its control to contain and 'own' them, or the magician decides that their personal experience is 'the way' for all others. They then seek to enforce their dogma on the rest of the line to ensure uniformity of thought, which is an act of power and control. This is why so much time is spent in the course looking at the complexities of power and control.

For this reason, when a mentored Quareia student completes their Adept training and is accepted as a Fellow of Quareia, they are not expected to conform to any set of rules, modes of behaviour, or trains of thought. They are accepted as they are; and they are also expected to accept every other Quareia adept, regardless of any differences of opinion. This sidesteps the issue of dogma creeping into a magical line, and allows plenty of room for evolution. Quareia adepts in Far Eastern countries, for example, will be different from Quareia adepts in the USA or Europe, as the cultural and social modes of thinking are so different, at least on the surface.

Religions, and particularly the Abrahamic religions, all have factions and splinter groups that each adhere to a different set of dogmas. Because a dogma is like an unbreachable brick wall, each faction believes that they are the 'true way,' and all the others are heretics and failures. Again, this is all about power and control. This pattern of behaviour can also be observed in some magical lines, particularly the Golden Dawn line of magic. Many factions in that line battle over who is the 'one true line,' and whose myths and dogmas are correct.

This happens when students and adepts (or followers, in a religion) are not fully immersed in the direct experience of contact, and access to any such contact is restricted to a select few. This sets up a hierarchy of control and power, which ultimately locks people out and away from the direct experience of deep magic.

As you go through your training, you will learn the dynamics of cause and effect in magic, as well as certain rules and set behaviours that are rooted in cause and effect. These are not the same as dogmas: they are mutable, and as each magical generation develops and matures, the cause and effect dynamic of magic shifts. It constantly evolves, just as the people who come into a magical line also constantly evolve and change as generations develop and change. The way you learn Quareia magic, and the way someone in a hundred years will learn Quareia magic, will be different. Dogma would stop this development and change, which is why it is really important to understand the dynamics of dogma, and the allure of a set of immovable absolutes which give a sense of continuation and predictability. Don't fall into the dogma trap as an adept, and understand fully the uniqueness of your own development and understanding.

8.5 What if you are an adherent of a specific religion?

Magic is about two things: learning about yourself in great depth, and learning about how the universe around you works, from an inner magical perspective. Through learning about those two things, you learn how to become a player in the production instead of a passive recipient. Really this is the difference between a magician and a non-magician: a magician is about action and intent.

When a magician is young or immature, they stride out to use action and intent to change their world for themselves. If they are successful, they may become curious about how and why their success happened. That brings them face to face with consciousness and beings that are not human like themselves. The experience is a bit like coming face to face with your first elephant as it crashes out of the jungle. The elephant and you look at each other, the elephant thinks, "oh shit, not again," and you think, "woah, that is one big dude... what the hell is that?"

Having made that connection, a slow series of steps takes the magician in ever-widening circles, like ripples on a pond, until they start to bump up against the power of Divinity—the power and presence of God within everything. At first the magician does not know how to connect with that power, or even what it is. But in time their encounters become more and more powerful and meaningful until, one day, the magician realizes they are connecting with Divinity in their own unique way, not through any religious pattern. That is when the magician flowers as a mystic, and the mystic flowers as a magician. Neither religion nor belief comes into it at all: it is simply a real, powerful, practical experience that they will never, ever forget.

Once the magician has experienced Divinity in their unique one-to-one way, they begin to see fragments of what they experienced in the religious and mystical writings of others: mystics, priests, priestesses, poets, artists, hermits... It is irrelevant what religion they are, as the baseline of the experience is the same. But in order to recognize it, to truly recognize it in the writings of others, you have to experience it for yourself. You cannot theorize or read about it and think you 'know.' You don't.

The experience comes from the slow unpeeling of the magician that results from their gradual steps through the cold waters of magic. Any type of magic, just like any religion, can bring a person to this point, if the potential is within them. But if the potential is not there, then no amount of studying magical systems or immersion in religion will trigger it. It is a latent 'something' that is either already there, or not. It is in most people drawn to magic by some strange compulsion, a memory, some voice, or through dreams. Usually magic calls such people in their childhood, then waits for them to catch up.

Some magical leaders have claimed that a magician must have a religion, because the most important magical path is to develop a relationship with Divinity and work with it. This is the other stumbling block that magicians may be tripping over when they feel that religion is a must for magic. A *deity* is a *god*, like Amun, Durga, Isis, Christ, or Thor. A *deity* is not *Divinity*; Divinity flows through deities. Deities are aspects and substations of creation, all of which are expressions of Divinity. Understanding the difference between having a relationship with the Divine, and being part of a religion, is paramount in magic: one does not necessarily include the other.

For a magician, a religion is viewed specifically as an operating system that functions between the magician and Divinity, an operating system that can be worked with when necessary. It is important that magicians know how a religion works from an inner as well as outer perspective, and understands the construction, energetic expression and collective consciousness of that religion. Through that knowledge, the magician can operate from within that religion if it is necessary, and can then back out afterwards – and remember, they are backing away from the structure, the man-made religion, not from Divinity itself. That is only possible if the magician fully understands that religions are simply constructs, and to gain that understanding, they need to be exposed to more than one religion, more than one operating system in their training. Through such exposure, and working from the inside of that system and then backing out, the magician can begin to understand the layers of complexity within construction, and apply that knowledge in their own work.

Divinity existed before religion and will exist after humanity has ceased to be. Divinity can flow into religions, and can reach out through deities and humans alike. Divinity is the consciousness behind creation, and the consciousness that flows through all creation. Most religions have a special designation for Divinity, above and beyond their deities. Often Divinity is expressed as the 'unseen,' or 'unknowable' one. In magic, Divine power is present in everything we do, and in everything around us, waiting until we stumble blindly into its presence, which opens our awareness. As a power it is neither good nor bad: it is simply *necessary*.

If you are an adherent to a specific religion, and wish to develop in depth in magic, then you will have to divorce yourself from the belief that your way is right and all other ways and religions are wrong. You will also have to put your religious identity to one side on occasions and immerse yourself in, and learn from, other religions without thinking that you are betraying yours. Nor must you succumb to the dogmatic idea that doing this would be acting contrary to the 'laws of God.'

God, Divinity, is everywhere and in everything. Religion is simply a man-made mechanism for communion between us and God. Once you move that mechanism of communion aside, then you will see how all the dogma is simply control, social structure, and boundaries to provide a group identity. Learn to wear your religion lightly, while deepening your relationship with the Divine through both your religion and your magical work. If everything about your religion—identity, outfits, bells, rituals, dogmas—is important to you, then it is not God you are looking for, but a *home* that you can identify with. Understand that for yourself by learning to *know yourself*, because without knowing yourself, you cannot know the Divine.

The swimmer in the Nu is one with the darkness and silence. The swimmer does not know he is a swimmer: he is and is within the Nu. The golden rays of Re fall upon the swimmer, lighting up that which was in darkness. The swimmer reflects the light of Re, and is thus no longer one with the Nu.

Summary

Here is a list of basic things to remember and answers to simple, technical questions.

- Remember to always take notes.

- Save all your essays and research as Word documents, so that it can all be submitted to Quareia should you wish to be mentored or included in Quareia community groups. And make sure you regularly back up your files. (If you cannot afford to buy Word then you can use a free, open source alternative like Libreoffice that can produce Word files.)

- Be adaptable, and use your common sense. If you cannot stand in ritual then sit in a chair. Whenever you need to adapt something out of real necessity, look carefully at the action that needs adapting and make sure that your modification will still be functional for its magical purpose. If elements are being used—fire, water, earth—then make sure you still use those elements. And electricity is neither fire nor flame!

- When you get stuck, self-question and search for an answer yourself. Make your own decisions: do not expect others to decide things for you. You are bound to make some mistakes—that is normal. Just learn from them.

- There is no race, but there is rhythm. Work at a pace that works around your life, but do keep working. Slow and steady is better than cramming, then doing nothing for months.

- Don't expect to understand everything fully, particularly in the Apprentice section. It is okay not to understand things: understanding dawns in its own time. The Mysteries can be complicated, and they unfold according to their own schedule. Realize that a lot of the territory you will cover will be entirely new for you, and just keep moving forward.

- Don't be tempted to change the ritual patterns or visions to suit yourself. Everything is as it is for a good reason. If you change the structure—for example, changing the directions or tools used, or bits of the visions—then it will lock you out of the system.

- In light of the two above comments, keep an open mind.

- Remember, simply reading a lesson is not doing it! If you skip any practical work, then you will not have gained the experience, understanding, and inner transformation that you need to develop and progress. The Mysteries are learned by doing, not by studying. Studying is for filling the gaps in your surface knowledge; the Magical Mysteries are triggered by actual work.

- Enjoy it. Don't treat the course as some terrible thing that must be overcome as quickly as possible. It is a long and winding path, so enjoy the views and the companions that you will discover on the way.

- *The Quareia Magician's Deck* is not used formally until the Initiate section, but if you wish to explore it while you are still an apprentice, then it will not harm your training. Just try not to terrify yourself with it!

- *The Book of Gates* is not required reading, but it is suggested. It would be most helpful for people at the Adept level of training. But if it interests you before you get there, then nothing is stopping you from studying it.

- With ritual baths, if you do not have access to a bath then use a bucket of water. Wash your face, each foot, and all of your body that you can reach. Pay attention to the back of your neck, then pour water over your head and back. Be careful to make sure every part of you has been cleansed.

- If you are not a native English speaker and have problems understanding some of the course's terminology, then check out the Facebook Quareia Magical Discussion group, which is open to anyone doing or interested in Quareia. It has people from all over the world, and someone there may be able to help. Otherwise, take note of what you do not understand, research the word or phrase if you can, or come back to it later. You may find as you progress that your understanding of the term begins to develop. If you are reading a translation of Quareia in a different language, then be aware that it may not be a good or accurate translation. There are many subtle undertones used in the language of this course, so bear that in mind.

- When you truly do not understand something, or there is a particular working that you truly cannot do at the present time, then move forward with the intent of going back and revisiting it in the near future.

- Don't overthink or overanalyze something, or obsess over a simple action. It can be tempting to overthink something and end up tied in knots over a simple detail, like the exact direction of a door, or which Rider-Waite deck to use (they are all the same—who cares?!). Learn to be mutable, and try not to control every little detail.

- Keep a sense of humour. It is one of the most valuable things in magic.

I do nothing but go about persuading you all, old and young alike, not to take thought for your persons or your properties, but and chiefly to care about the greatest improvement of the soul. I tell you that virtue is not given by money, but that from virtue comes money and every other good of man, public as well as private. This is my teaching, and if this is the doctrine which corrupts the youth, I am a mischievous person.

 — *Plato,* Apologia *(29d), recounting the words of Socrates at his trial.*

9 781911 134329

Printed in March 2021
by Rotomail Italia S.p.A., Vignate (MI) - Italy